C000053208

Richard Stern is consultant psychiat[
London, and honorary senior lecturei
school there. He trained in psychiatry at the Institute of Psychiatry and Maudsley Hospital, London, and received his doctorate
in medicine from London University in 1972, which involved a
treatment study of agoraphobia. As senior lecturer on research
projects into therapeutic studies, he helped to develop new treatments for agoraphobia and for obsessive-compulsive disorders.
Since joining St George's Hospital in 1979 he has, in his role as
consultant psychiatrist, worked in the field of general psychiatry
while maintaining a life-long interest in phobic disorders. He has
been a Fellow of the Royal College of Psychiatrists since 1986.
He supervises trainee psychiatrists in behavioural and cognitive
psychotherapy. His book *Behavioural Techniques* was published
in 1978 and he co-authored *The Practice of Behavioural and
Cognitive Psychotherapy* (1991). In addition he has published
forty scientific and scholarly articles in the field of psychological
treatments.

Richard Stern is married and lives with his wife and two sons
in south London.

Mastering Phobias

Cases, Causes and Cures

Richard Stern

PENGUIN BOOKS

PENGUIN BOOKS

Published by the Penguin Group
Penguin Books Ltd, 27 Wrights Lane, London w8 5TZ, England
Penguin Books USA Inc., 375 Hudson Street, New York, New York 10014, USA
Penguin Books Australia Ltd, Ringwood, Victoria, Australia
Penguin Books Canada Ltd, 10 Alcorn Avenue, Toronto, Ontario, Canada M4V 3B2
Penguin Books (NZ) Ltd, 182–190 Wairau Road, Auckland 10, New Zealand

Penguin Books Ltd, Registered Offices: Harmondsworth, Middlesex, England

Published in Penguin Books 1995
1 3 5 7 9 10 8 6 4 2

Filmset by Datix International Limited, Bungay, Suffolk
Printed in England by Clays Ltd, St Ives plc
Set in 10/12pt Times Monophoto

For Susan, David and Jonathan

Contents

How I came to be interested in phobias. My research into agoraphobia. The historical development from primitive behavioural approaches in simple phobic problems to cognitive treatment in more complex ones. The revolutionary impact of the behavioural and cognitive treatments combined. The natural course of phobias. How common are phobias? Are phobias inherited? Do phobic patients have other problems? Can psychological theories explain phobias?

Agoraphobia: the housebound housewife syndrome. Cases I have treated, including 'the girl who could not go out', showing the real degree of disability these patients experience.

Social phobia and how it differs from agoraphobia. How common is it? How is it caused? What conditions it must be distinguished from, such as some kinds of major mental illness. Cases of social phobia, including a young man socially crippled by it. Serious problems of anger and blushing.

A variety of cases of animal phobias: spider, snake and dog phobias.

Classification of phobias. Thunder, disease, flying, blood, death, gaining weight, bridge, being enclosed and farting phobias.

Sexual fears and fantasies, and the pressure of sexual performance. Problems specific to women: vaginismus; anorgasmia. Definition and treatment by masturbatory techniques. The principle of sensate focus in self-treatment. Problems specific to men: difficulties with erection and the use of sensate focus; premature

ejaculation and the use of the 'stop–start' technique; failure of
ejaculation and the use of masturbatory techniques. General
points about sexual phobias.

Cautionary tales: do not jump to the conclusion that you have a
phobia. Medical humility: doctors get it wrong at times. Cases
illustrating how it might be a physical problem, depression or
obsessive-compulsive disorder. When a correct assessment has
been made, the many possible treatments for phobia-like symptoms, some of them medical and some involving life-style
adjustments.

Some drugs can make the action of behavioural therapy
stronger, and are of value in cases that would otherwise present
obstacles to treatment. Certain classes of medications can help
some aspects of phobic disorders some of the time. These are the
minor tranquillizers, some kinds of antidepressant and beta-
blockers.

How to tell if you have agoraphobia or social phobia, one of the
specific phobias or a sexual one. The use of flow charts and
questionnaires to indicate if the problem is serious and what can
be done to help.

Details of self-help programmes: for people with agoraphobia
who cannot leave the house; for those with social phobias: how
to set objectives and how these may have to be limited and
realistic; for those who lack social skills or lack assertion. Lack
of impulse control can be helped by anger management.

How to contact self-help groups run by fellow-sufferers. How
and when to seek professional help from the various medical,
psychological and counselling bodies. Relaxation exercises.

Acknowledgements

This book draws upon several case histories previously described, often in a slightly different form, in *The Practice of Behavioural and Cognitive Psychotherapy* (1991), published by Cambridge University Press and co-written with my colleague Dr Lynne Drummond. The cases of Jeffrey, June, Adrian, Lorraine and Michael are from this source with the generous permission of Lynne Drummond and Cambridge University Press.

The author would also like to thank Sigmund Freud Copyrights and the Institute of Psycho-Analysis and The Hogarth Press for permission to quote from the case of Frau Emmy von N. from *The Standard Edition of the Complete Psychological Works of Sigmund Freud*, Volume II (translated by James and Alix Strachey).

1 Phobia: The Irrational Fear

Most of us are scared of something. Phobic people have been described as extremely intelligent people behaving stupidly. This book is for those who, at first, may be too scared or embarrassed to seek professional help. It tells you how to help yourself and, by describing many different kinds of phobias, what professionals can do for you.

My own interest in phobias began about twenty-five years ago with a simple idea: phobias are just like the fears everybody has, only they are more severe – although I now realize that there is a bit more to it than that. After I completed my psychiatric training, followed by several years of research at the Maudsley Hospital in London, I have worked since 1979 as a psychiatrist at St George's Hospital. In my day-to-day work, now as a consultant psychiatrist, I teach medical students and trainee psychiatrists, and see the whole range of psychiatric illnesses. Patients with a fascinating variety of phobic and anxiety problems have provided me with case material for this book. In all instances, names and biographical details have been changed to protect their identity.

Anyone who has been to an interview, sat an examination, or seen a Hitchcock movie has experienced fear. So, when I first began work as a young psychiatrist, I thought that this group of patients would be easy to identify with. At this time, in the 1960s, a new and exciting psychological therapy called behaviour therapy was being developed. Behaviour therapy can be defined as a group of treatments with the central hypothesis that psychological distress results from learned behaviour and can therefore be unlearned. This treatment was being applied on an experimental basis to patients with specific phobias of spiders or of animals such as cats and dogs.

I was soon to learn the important difference between these patients and people with normal fears: with phobias the fear is *irrational*. There is no reason to fear spiders in this country as no dangerous varieties exist here. Patients with spider phobia know this but will still run a mile if you put a spider in front of them, and they will avoid situations where spiders may be present. The irrationality of the fear and the avoidance of the phobic object are now considered crucial for the definition of a phobia.

In 1971 some dramatic and crucial experiments, which I was fortunate to be involved in, were carried out at the Maudsley Hospital and were subsequently published.[1] Phobic patients were asked to try to *stay* in the very phobic situation they were frightened of. A spider phobic patient was to try to remain in a room while a small spider, securely enclosed in a jam jar, was brought in and placed some distance from him. He agreed to this and then, a little later, for the jar to be moved slightly closer. Within an hour the patient surprised us all by agreeing to have the jar on his lap. He was wired up to a measuring device called a polygraph, which gave us a readout of his pulse rate and, in addition, could monitor the arousal of his nervous system. Not surprisingly, his heart rate was very high at first, but within half an hour it had declined and at the end of an hour it was more or less normal. There was a short rise in heart rate each time the jar was brought closer, but a return to normal when the patient had got used to the new situation. A similar picture was seen with the measurement of nervous system arousal. This *getting used to* the situation in physiological terms is given the scientific term habituation (from the French *habituer*). In the second treatment session the patient allowed the spider to be taken from the jar, and once again went through his habituation process. After two more sessions he was cured.

There was a buzz of excitement from psychiatrists at these results, but at the same time many of us were extremely sceptical. It was one thing treating a few spider phobic and dog phobic patients, but these were not really representative of the majority of phobic problems facing psychiatrists. The most common phobia presenting to psychiatrists was agoraphobia and surveys suggested that the number of people with this condition was considerable and that these patients were *very* disabled.

Agoraphobia is the fear of open spaces, crowded places and

most forms of public transport. These situations cannot simply be put in a jam jar! The next best thing is to have the patient *imagine* them in the clinic – the basis of a technique used in the 1950s by an American psychiatrist, Joseph Wolpe. He called this approach systematic desensitization.[2] Wolpe thought that if people were made to relax during gradual exposure to a fearful stimulus, they would not experience fear at the same time. The idea behind this was that two incompatible emotions cannot be felt simultaneously: you cannot easily laugh and cry together. The technique of systematic desensitization involves teaching a patient how to relax their whole body, then to imagine being near to what they fear. This takes six to twelve sessions, after which the patient is encouraged to face the situation in real life, beginning with the least difficult task and gradually working up to the most difficult. Despite its effectiveness, systematic desensitization was a very time-consuming therapy. Could we apply the newer treatments of rapid exposure devised for spider (and other specific phobias) to the huge clinical problem of agoraphobia?

Psychiatrists, used to sitting in their offices waiting for patients to visit by appointment, now had to work in the field and in 1972 I was funded by the Medical Research Council to carry out a treatment study into agoraphobia. The question under investigation came from those habituation experiments carried out on animals, which predicted that habituation would occur only if the animal were exposed to the phobic situation for long enough. They also predicted that short periods of exposure to the phobic situation would make the phobia *worse*. When this was applied to agoraphobic patients it meant comparing the results of taking an agoraphobic patient on the bus for two hours with taking them, say, on four separate expeditions of half an hour, so that the *total* time on the bus was the same for the two groups. As with the spider phobic patient, the heart rate was also monitored but with a portable, pulse rate measuring-gadget which the patient carried in a small case.

We were now out of the laboratory, out of the clinic, and in the real world which agoraphobic patients find so hard to cope with. Just how hard was illustrated by an incident in which I

stood at the top of an escalator with a patient during a behavioural therapy session. All had gone reasonably well in the
session which, in the event, turned out to be the last one. The
patient, a young man in his twenties, had a panic attack and
said, 'There is *no* way I am going down there!', and threw the
case with the valuable measuring equipment down the escalator
stairs. He ran home and when I spoke to him later on the
telephone declined any further treatment. I have been unable to
find out what happened to him.

Fortunately, most cases in the study were not as difficult.
Sixteen patients carried out the behavioural programme in a
way that allowed me to compare the effects of two hours'
exposure to the phobic situation with a series of four thirty-
minute exposures.[3] The results clearly showed the advantage of
the longer sessions and to this day underpin the importance of
duration of exposure in the treatment of agoraphobia.

Other researchers have attempted to make the treatment easier
and more helpful still. One idea was to try the effects of sedative
drugs *combined* with behavioural therapy and these controversial
studies are reviewed in chapter 8 'The Role of Medication'.
Another idea was to combine the behavioural therapy with
antidepressant drugs; where the drug imipramine has been used,
results are most encouraging.[4]

Over the years, the refinement of psychological treatment
factors in agoraphobia continued. It was thought that treatment
in groups would be more cost-effective as group therapy required
less professional time.[5] But, in practice, it is often difficult to get
a group of similar phobic patients together at the same moment
and progress of the group as a whole is linked to that of its
slowest member. My father, who was a naval officer in the
Second World War, told me that the Atlantic convoys had the
same problem: the fastest ships had to go more slowly for the
benefit of the convoy as a whole.

Another area of investigation was into marital and family
factors in the treatment of agoraphobia.[6] Aside from actual
work with the families and partners of phobic patients, the other
development has been home-based treatment where the patient
carries out instructions to face the feared situation on his or her

own. This may sound surprising because the hallmark of agoraphobia is that patients will not go out alone. However, we now know that in an emergency such as a fire, patients *will* run out of the house rather than be burnt to death. In addition, some trials of drug therapy in agoraphobia were difficult to explain. Patients in a placebo group, that is to say with a dummy drug, improved when clearly they should not have done. The explanation was that patients in the trial, unbeknown to the investigators, had spoken to other patients who told them that if they tried as hard as they could to go out for as long as possible, it seemed to help. They had done just that and as a result improved.

How crucial it is to treat both partners in an agoraphobia case is shown by an early experience. The patient, whom I saw on her own, was a married woman with no children. The behavioural therapy was progressing well: after four sessions she was able to go into a shopping mall which had been impossible for her. Then I received a telephone call along the following lines from the woman's irate husband: 'I don't want my wife to have any more of your treatment. I don't like her going out spending money. I like her to be at home so that I can be sure where she is all of the time.' This sad patient later telephoned to apologize for her husband's action but never returned for treatment. We have now learned not to proceed with behavioural treatments without at least one joint session with the patient's partner.

Most of the treatments described so far come under the term behaviour therapy and are supported by careful scientific controlled treatment trials. In the 1970s these purely behavioural approaches were criticized by a newly emerging school of psychology: cognitive therapy. This school of thought was generally critical of the fact that behavioural treatments seemed to ignore common sense. As the philosopher of science Karl Popper stated: 'Science is only common sense writ large', and so it seemed to make sense to explore the work of these cognitive pioneers to see if their ideas could be incorporated into the treatment of phobic patients.[7] One of the cognitive therapists was the American psychologist Albert Ellis who wrote:

Overconcern about a dangerous situation usually leads to your exaggerating the chances of it actually occurring. Thus, if you are terribly frightened about taking an airplane trip, you will probably imagine that there is an excellent possibility of your plane getting into a serious accident when, actually, there is about one in a hundred thousand chances of it doing so. Even though your worry, in such an instance, has some real grounds for existing, it by no means has the unrealistically exaggerated grounds that you, by your overconcern, create.[8]

Along similar lines, the American psychiatrist Aaron Beck pointed out in 1967 that cognitive therapy can help patients use problem-solving techniques to correct distortions of thinking based on mistaken beliefs.[9] Beck's early work in cognitive therapy was devised to help patients suffering from depression, and it became clear that working at the cognitive level in combination with a behavioural approach made a great deal of sense. It was impossible to work with patients without considering their ideas: the way they looked at the world in general and, in particular, the way they 'talked to themselves' – their internal dialogue when they were about to face a fearful situation. The usual finding was that patients said what made them worse, such as, 'This fear is going to kill me.' It was this thought that could lead to the avoidant behaviour which is the distinguishing feature of phobias.

From about 1990 therapists trained in behavioural psychotherapy began to talk to those who had trained with Ellis and Beck, and to develop a treatment that combined *both* aspects. When reading the cognitive theories of Beck, I realized that I had been incorporating similar ideas into my own work for some years, rather as the character in Molière's play *Le Bourgeois gentilhomme* discovered that he had been speaking prose all his life. One outcome of this new synthesis was my book *The Practice of Behavioural and Cognitive Psychotherapy*, co-written with Dr Lynne Drummond, for trainee therapists.

Phobias are the most treatable of the severe nervous problems: my aim is to make people aware of this. I have learned both from successes and failures in the treatment of phobic patients and continue to learn from my patients. There is much more to discover before we can answer even the simplest questions often asked by phobic patients. For example, What is the cause of phobias? What part, if any, is inherited? How and why does psychological treatment work? Let us start by seeing what happens if phobias are allowed to run their natural course.[10]

The natural course of phobias

The course of phobic disorders is one of remissions and relapses of varying durations. At the start of the phobia a short episode may clear up completely after a few days or weeks, but once severe phobias have been present for a year or more, partial rather than total remissions seem to be the usual outcome until later life. In a survey carried out by the Open Door, a self-help group for agoraphobia, only 20 per cent reported periods of complete remission after the initial onset of the phobia.

How common are phobias?

Agoraphobia accounts for 60 per cent of phobias. At least two thirds of agoraphobics are women, usually between fifteen and thirty-five years old. When the condition has been present for more than a year, it runs a fluctuating course with minor remissions and relapses over many years. The prevalence of phobic disorders varies greatly across different studies[11] and depending on the setting: general practice, general hospital and psychiatric outpatient studies all show different rates.

The major community survey was carried out in Canada in the late sixties. From a sample of 325, the current prevalence of phobias as a whole was 7.7 per cent, of illness/injury phobias 3.1 per cent, of agoraphobia 0.6 per cent, and of severe phobias only 0.2 per cent. Consequently, the frequency of a condition in psychiatric practice is not a good guide to its prevalence in the general population. In the Canadian study agoraphobia constituted only 8 per cent of all phobics but fully 50 per cent of treated phobics.

In the USA in the mid eighties a huge study was undertaken

of the rates and risks for psychiatric disorders based on a sample of over eighteen thousand adults aged eighteen years and over, living in five communities. In three communities, in which the total sample was 11,506, the pooled six-month prevalence rate was 0.8 per cent for panic, 3.8 per cent for agoraphobia, 1.7 per cent for social phobia and 7 per cent for specific phobias. Rates were highest at ages twenty-five to forty-four, and lowest above the age of sixty-four.

Are phobias inherited?

'My mother [or my aunt] had terrible agoraphobia. Does this mean I will get it?' is a question often asked by relatives of phobic patients. To answer them means looking at genetic studies, most of which centre around agoraphobia.[12] One study, carried out in 1983, found that relatives of agoraphobics were at increased risk not only for agoraphobia but also for panic disorder. Another study looked at the familial risk of agoraphobia by questionnaire and interview, and found that patients with phobias tended to have either a parent or a sibling affected but not both; the risk to parents was not less than that to children, contrary to what some investigators expected.

Why agoraphobia runs in families, and especially among female relatives, is still unclear. The standard investigative technique here is to carry out *twin* studies where identical twins (monozygotic) are compared to non-identical (dizygotic) twins. Monozygotic twins have identical genetic material, whereas dizygotic ones are no more alike than any brothers or sisters would be. Harris *et al.* (1983) found that relatives of agoraphobics were at increased risk not only for agoraphobia but also for panic disorder and for other phobias, while those with relatives suffering panic disorder had only a raised risk of panic disorder. Moran and Andrews (1985) studied the familial risk of agoraphobia by questionnaire and interview, and found that probands (those forming the starting-point for the genetic study of a family) tended to have either a parent or a sibling affected, not both; the risk to parents was not less than that to children, contrary to what would be expected with transmission from a single recessive gene. The familial prevalence of agoraphobia is unlikely to result from copying the behaviour of family members as most of the probands had never met a sufferer: of the probands 85 per cent came from a family in which neither parent was reported to be agoraphobic.

A high rate of phobic disorders was found among mothers (31 per cent), along with an increase in other neuroses among both parents (55 per cent of mothers, 24 per cent of fathers) (Solyom et al., 1974), and a higher than expected rate of school phobia among the children (14 per cent for ages eleven to fifteen) (Berg, 1976).

In a family study of agoraphobia, panic disorder and non-anxious controls (twenty probands per group), the morbidity risk for all anxiety disorders among first-degree relatives was respectively: 32, 33 and 15 per cent; the risk for relatives of controls being lower (Harris et al., 1983).

Why agoraphobia runs in families, and especially among female relatives, is still unclear. Among twins with panic disorder or agoraphobia, anxiety disorders were more than five times as frequent in monozygotic as dizygotic co-twins (Torgerson, 1983). Carey (1982) studied twenty-one twin probands with phobic disorders; of these seven of the eight monozygotic co-twins had either a phobic disorder or phobic features, compared with only five of the thirteen dizygotic co-twins. This is likely to be a genetic rather than a learned effect as even twins raised apart were concordant. Also in at least two of the concordant monozygotic pairs the type of phobia present in one twin was unknown to the other.

Of the other phobic disorders a remarkable fact has emerged about one of the specific phobias: blood-injury phobia. Of patients with this condition, 68 per cent had biological relatives who were blood phobic, a rate three to six times higher than the frequency of corresponding phobias among the relatives of agora-phobics or social phobics (Marks, 1969). It had been suggested that the strong family history might mean that blood-injury originates in a genetically determined extreme autonomic response. This group is also unusual in that the response to the phobic stimulus is bradycardia rather than the more usual

tachycardia. Bradycardia leads patients to faint readily and may
give a predisposition to the phobia.

Do phobic patients have other problems?

If you have a severe phobia it is very understandable that you
will also get symptoms of depression: irritability, difficulty getting off to sleep, lack of energy and feelings of hopelessness. I
often see patients with symptoms both of depression and of
agoraphobia. Often the depression should be treated in its own
right and this should be discussed with your doctor. In most
cases of agoraphobia, the phobic symptoms are then left. However, in patients prone to both conditions, agoraphobia can be
made worse during a depressive episode.

Depersonalization and derealization can occur in agoraphobia. In these strange states the patient feels unreal and disem-
bodied. The phenomenon is called depersonalization when it
refers to the patient, and derealization when it refers to the sur-
roundings. A distinct syndrome, the phobic anxiety depersonalization syndrome,[13] has been discovered in which 80 per cent
of cases had agoraphobia, along with other symptoms said to
indicate an abnormality in that part of the brain called the
temporal lobe. It has not, however, been proven that patients
with agoraphobia and depersonalization also have temporal lobe
disorder.

Generalized anxiety is common in agoraphobia and may be
constant or variable.[14] Panic attacks, though, may be very
dramatic and are often the reason precipitating consultation.
There is great variability in the frequency of general anxiety and
panics: in some studies 33 per cent of patients did not have
panic attacks but in other studies 70 per cent did not. The major
diagnostic manual used in the USA distinguishes between agoraphobia with panic attacks and those cases without.

Apart from agoraphobia, the phobia responsible for other
problems is social phobia. Not surprisingly, it leads to problems
in making relationships which can result in social isolation, itself
a cause of depression, and lack of personal fulfilment.

Can psychological theories explain phobias?

In one of his early case studies (1889) Sigmund Freud described the fascinating case of Frau Emmy von N., a forty-year-old woman, whom he treated with hypnosis, the fashionable treatment of the moment:

> Under hypnosis she explained that her fear of worms came from her once having been given a present of a pretty pincushion; but next morning, when she wanted to use it, a lot of little worms had crept out of it, because it had been filled with bran which was not quite dry . . .
>
> Once, she said, when she had been walking with her husband in a park in St Petersburg, the whole path leading to a pond had been covered with toads, so that they had to turn back. There had been times when she had been unable to hold out her hand to anyone, for fear of it turning into a dreadful animal, as had so often happened. I tried to free her from her fear of animals by going through them one by one and asking her if she was afraid of them. In the case of some of them she answered 'no'; in the case of others, 'I mustn't be afraid of them.'[15]

At this point Freud makes a fascinating footnote: *'The procedure I was following here can scarcely be regarded as a good one; none of it was carried out exhaustively enough.'* Today cognitive-behavioural therapy recognizes that the thorough facing-up to the phobic situation for a prolonged period is crucial. The above quotation illustrates that Freud was far less doctrinaire in his treatments of phobias than is commonly believed.

In the nineteenth century psychoanalysts stressed the importance of symbolism in the generation of phobic disorders. In a classic case described by Freud, five-year-old Hans developed a phobia of horses after witnessing an accident involving a horse while out walking with his father. Freud proposed that the horse symbolized a feared retaliation from his father. A later psychoanalyst Fenichel explained Freud's views:

If an individual no longer feels threatened by his father but by a horse, he can avoid hating his father; here the distortion was a way out of the conflict of ambivalence. The father, who had been hated and loved simultaneously, is loved only, and the hatred is displaced on to the bad horse. Freud also brings to our attention that a boy is forced to associate with his father every day, whereas the threatening horse can be avoided by simply not going outdoors.[16]

In a subsequent theoretical framework Freud viewed phobic disorders as resulting from conflicts centred on unresolved child-hood sexual situations. Freud gives an example of a patient with a phobia of boats which was attributed to sexual feelings towards her father in childhood: 'From these observations, it was clear that, through the mechanism of displacement and because of their association with the sexual activity that had initially aroused her anxiety, boats had come to be the symbol of the patient's sexual conflict, which was manifested clinically as a simple phobia.'

One variant of the theme of unconscious motivation, held more recently, is that patients with agoraphobia are really suffer-ing from something wrong in their sexual relationships. The phobic behaviour is seen as a means of expressing or coping with aspects of an unsatisfactory sexual relationship. A more likely explanation, however, is that anxiety caused by sexual conflict may increase the probability of panic attacks, and high neuroticism may lead both to conflict in the relationship and poor response to treatment. Nevertheless, relationship factors should not be disregarded in treatment: I have already quoted from the case where the husband stopped treatment for agora-phobia because he did not want his wife to go out shopping without him. Clearly marital assessment is important before individual treatment of a phobia is started.

In the 1920s psychologists in the USA turned to conditioned reflex theories to explain the origin of phobias. John B. Watson described the famous case of Albert, an eleven-month-old baby, who was systematically exposed to a whole battery of objects such as rats, rabbits, dogs and a variety of masks, and showed no concern with these. However, when Albert was shown a white rat and *simultaneously* an iron bar was struck on a metal object behind his head, Albert withdrew from the rat.

Seven days later, when Albert was shown the rat unaccompanied by the noise, he showed a fear response, which the experimenters claimed to be a *conditioned response.* Seventeen days later the response was noted to have waned, but it was strengthened by a further banging of the bar in the presence of the rat. One month later Albert was observed to have a strong fear response to rats, dogs, fur coats and a mask of Santa Claus with a long beard. Unfortunately no follow-up of Albert's progress was reported, so claims which were made as a result of this case are hard to take seriously.

Both psychodynamic and conditioned reflex theories have been supplanted for different reasons. Psychodynamic theories are difficult to support or disprove, but when ingenious studies have been conducted they have failed to confirm the theories: the idea that boys desire to replace their fathers as their mothers' lovers has found no support in a variety of studies. Watson's conditioned reflex experiments were easy to repeat, and the early results were *not* replicated and phobias were not produced in infants subjected to similar experiments. The search was on for new theories to explain both how phobias are caused and what keeps them going.

Since the 1950s theories derived from the psychology of learning have underpinned advances in the understanding of phobias and in behavioural treatments. It is worth emphasizing that there is no *one* theory of learning: there are a number of different theories which have developed over the years, and some have proved of greater influence than others. Phobic patients rarely test the reality of their fears but characteristically avoid the phobic situation. One way knowledge has advanced is by the study of rat behaviour in the laboratory. A rat can be made to show phobic-like behaviour which enables us to study how it happens and how to cure it. Morrie Baum, a psychologist working in Canada, devised the Baum box, a cage with a floor which can be made painful to the rat by passing a small electric charge through it.[17] There is a ledge built into the side of the box and after a short while the rat learns to jump on to this ledge to escape the shock. Then the shock is switched off. But the rat jumps up on the ledge *whenever* it is put in the Baum box even though it no longer receives a shock. (This behaviour is analogous to the avoidance that phobic patients show.) Then the experimenter does something rather nasty from the rat's point of view: the ledge is removed from the box so that the rat has no way of avoiding exposure to the floor. Some rats soon learn in this way to overcome their fear, but in others the fear and avoidance response lasts longer. These are like agoraphobia sufferers who avoid going out long after a panic attack has occurred. These difficult rats can be 'treated' by inserting a paddle into the box and gently pushing the rat out to explore the floor. This is similar to taking an agoraphobic patient by the hand and encouraging them to venture outside. The avoidance conditioning model of fear acquisition may give some indication of how experiments with rats can help in understanding the cause of phobias and how they can be treated.

We have come a long way since the turn of the century where the predominant idea was that phobias were caused by unconscious factors. Simple conditioning theories have also not withstood the test of time, but more complex ones involving avoidance learning are helpful in our understanding, as are those from cognitive psychology. An integration of these last two has been responsible for modern behavioural and cognitive psychotherapy, the basis of this book.

2 Agoraphobia

Like one, that on a lonesome road
Doth walk in fear and dread,
And having once turned round walks on,
And turns no more his head;
Because he knows, a frightful fiend
Doth close behind him tread.

— Coleridge,
'The Rime of the Ancient Mariner'

Agoraphobia is also known as the housebound housewife syndrome. This may sound rather sexist but the fact is that most sufferers are female and married. The word agoraphobia implies that the fear is of the outside world since the Greek root *agora* means an assembly place or marketplace and *phobos* means fear. The agora in Athens today still serves its ancient function of meeting-place. Agoraphobics fear and avoid such large open spaces, in addition to crowded places, and, also, the means to get to them if it involves public transport. Typically, an agoraphobic can travel by motor car but not by bus or train.

If you have agoraphobia and you go out, you may experience a variety of anxiety symptoms: sweating, palpitations, dizziness in the head and weakness in the legs. Breathing problems may take the form of difficulty in catching one's breath or, more commonly, too rapid breathing known as hyperventilation. Panic attacks of such anxiety can last from a few minutes to several hours, and patients have a variety of underlying fears about what might happen to them during such an attack of panic. A common fear is that they will faint, make a fool of themselves in some way, or for others that they might go mad.

After such panic attacks phobic avoidance begins. Patients

who experience an attack in, say, the supermarket then stop going there. The next stage might be panic in the small corner shop, after which it too will be avoided. Then, if the patient has an attack just a hundred yards from home, she may stop going out altogether.

As well as total avoidance of panic-inducing situations, there are also some subtle kinds of avoidance individual patients develop such as total concentration on a book or newspaper to the extent that the external stimuli do not impinge. I have also known patients strike up an unremitting conversation with strangers on public transport towards the same end. Then there are patients who use classic counter-phobic activities such as wearing dark glasses, sucking strong-tasting sweets, going out only in the rain or in the dark, sticking to small alleyways and avoiding crossing roads, holding on to objects such as a shopping trolley, a dog on a leash or a pram (with or without a baby). They may also carry bottles of tablets or flasks of favourite alcoholic drinks, though usually they don't actually consume these. Several of my patients carry a card with my name, address and telephone number 'in case of emergency', although, to date, not one has needed to use it. These counter-phobic items are called *soteria* and are usually idiosyncratic.

In addition to the anxiety experienced facing the phobic situation, there is fear of the fear or anticipatory anxiety, also called phobophobia. Even thinking about going to the supermarket brings on symptoms. Patients who fear bus travel may cope if the bus comes straight-away, but if there is any delay fear builds up and they go home.

Agoraphobia was vividly described over a century ago by Westphal:

> Agony was much increased at those hours when the particular streets dreaded were deserted and the shops closed. The subjects experienced great comfort from the companionship of men or even an inanimate object, such as a vehicle or cane. The use of beer or wine also allowed the patient to pass through the feared locality with comparative comfort. One man even sought, without immoral motives, the companion-

ship of a prostitute as far as his own door ... some localities are more difficult of access than others; the patient walked far in order not to traverse the dreaded spaces ... in one instance the open country was less feared than sparsely housed streets in town. One case also had a dislike for crossing a certain bridge. He feared he would fall into the water. In this case, there also was apprehension of impending insanity.[1]

Things have not changed much, as shown by a case I saw recently.

The girl who could not go out

'Please see this 21-year-old woman who has been a prisoner in her own home for some time' read the letter of referral from Susan's general practitioner.

She herself explained: 'If I go anywhere out of the house I get so anxious that it feels as if I'm rooted to the spot. I also feel dizzy, I start to breathe too fast, my legs feel tense and my whole body goes rigid with fear. I feel as if I am not really there, but also everything around me seems unreal. It began about three years ago when I had a panic attack going for an interview. I did not get the post. Since then I've avoided going into crowded places. I could never go into a supermarket. I could not go on a bus or a train. Then it got so I could not go by car unless I was familiar with the driver. But for the last three years I have not been anywhere.'

Susan's problem was far from slight and she started individual psychotherapy a year after her agoraphobia began. 'The therapist said it was to do with my insecurity in childhood. I was expected to talk about that but most of the time the therapist said nothing. I did not know what to say, so I mostly sat in silence. Then he wanted to see me with my family. I think they were made to feel blame, as if it were all their fault. I thought it was all a waste of time and we stopped going.'

Susan had already read a self-help book on agoraphobia and was interested in the treatment called systematic desensitization: 'I like the idea of very gradually getting used to going outside again but, whatever else you do, no more psychotherapy – and I won't take any drugs.' I explained to Susan that systematic desensitization is considered nowadays to be rather old-fashioned. We no longer think it necessary to work through painstakingly long hierarchies (graduated lists), beginning with her *imagining* just going out one step from the safety of her home. Instead, I explained the principles of exposure therapy to her and she agreed to try a short walk to her friend's house, and to do this twice before her next appointment in two weeks' time.

At this meeting, she reported smilingly: 'That was so easy, it was frightening!' She did surprise herself by completing the homework task but all was not quite as straightforward as it seemed. She needed to go out at night (bright light is often a problem for agoraphobics); she had gone with her mother each time (companions make phobic situations more bearable); and her father had to take her home in the car from her friend's house.

Her next homework assignment was to try the same walk in daylight without her mother. This task was achieved: a small step for most people but an enormous one for Susan.

'So you went out alone for the first time in how long?'

'Three years. But I wasn't strictly alone . . . I had the dog with me.'

'What should you do next?'

'Do the same thing without the dog, I suppose?'

At this point the treatment seemed clear enough. Susan was to go out, increasing the distances from her home, alone whenever possible, to explore parks and supermarkets. All did not go according to plan and at the sixth session she reported: 'I am back to square one. My parents went away for the weekend and I stayed indoors. I started to think about what *might* happen if I did go out and this worked me up into a right state. I couldn't go anywhere.'

Susan was describing the anticipatory anxiety well known to behavioural-cognitive therapists. In simple terms this means that the more you think about something, the worse it gets. This therapy was not going to be as simple. One way to counteract anticipatory anxiety is to use the two-column technique where the patient makes a list of the feared consequences of going out in one column and rational responses in the other. An example in Susan's case was:

anticipatory anxiety	rational response
if I go out I'll collapse	when I did go out nothing happened
if I go out I'll get dizzy	I also get dizzy indoors but if I wait it goes
if I go out I'll die	I am still alive after my last venture out

At the end of six sessions along these lines, progress was still painfully slow. Susan got as far as attempting a train journey but had a panic attack on the railway platform: 'I just froze . . . It lasted only a few seconds. Then things around me looked unreal. I had a strange dizzy feeling. I felt as if I could not walk straight. This reduced my confidence about going out in general. Do you think I will ever get over this?'

My impression, which I discussed with Susan, was that she needed specific help with panic attacks at this stage and that it should be in the form of the medication more widely known in the treatment of depression: imipramine. She agreed, despite her earlier refusal, to start this medication, combined with the behavioural programme. After about three weeks, she was able once more to go for walks alone. She then agreed to go to a shopping centre for forty-five minutes and managed this without panic attacks.

The use of imipramine for panic disorders in the USA in the 1960s has been documented.[2] Yet no one really knew how it worked and why it should be successful for one patient and not for another. My experience was that it certainly did not work in all cases, but for Susan the effect was almost miraculous. She made dramatic progress and was soon able to go out to the park, her local shopping centre, and to travel by bus and train. When she came to the hospital without the assistance of her parents to tell me she had enrolled in college I knew that the improvement would be long-lasting. She had no need for imipramine after about six months.

Mary's story

Mary, a 35-year-old housewife, was travelling by bus to work, a journey of some twenty minutes to central London, when a panic attack occurred. She got off the bus at the next stop, hailed a passing taxi, and went straight home.

The following day she had anticipatory anxiety about going to work and pleaded with her husband to take her by car although it was inconvenient for him. He drove her to work for the rest of the week and after that a friend gave her a lift. She avoided bus travel until she gave up work to have children. Then she organized her husband to take her to the supermarket to avoid the bus journey there. He usually dropped her off at the entrance and picked her up at a pre-arranged time. One day when he did so, she was trembling with anxiety, having had a panic attack in the supermarket. After this she did all her provisioning at the corner shop. Despite the extra expense involved, her husband agreed to this as he found the regular chauffeuring tedious. Mary bought herself a shopping trolley, and felt confident enough gripping its handle. She soon noticed that she never went out without it, even if her purchases could be carried by hand. Later she found that she lacked the confidence to go out except on dark or rainy days when she followed a well-rehearsed route along small back streets, although it would have been quicker on the main road.

Mary's case illustrates many of the classic features of agoraphobia. But it also shows that not all cases respond to behavioural and cognitive therapy. After three sessions Mary's condition gradually deteriorated and led to increasing isolation and dependence on others, in particular her husband. She also had no confidence in social situations and avoided these. My hypothesis was that she and her husband needed her phobic symptoms for their marriage to work. She later made it clear to me that she did not really want to go through the discomfort of behavioural therapy and had only come at the instigation of a friend. Her husband did not want her to go on with treatment.

The Failures of Behaviour Therapy by the psychiatrist Edna Foa, with Paul Emmelkamp, is a collection of cases where, as with Mary, some factor stood in the way of successful treatment.[3] Some cases were those with serious marital discord, others with a depressive illness. Some patients had delusional ideas such as in major mental illness. For example, 'I cannot go out of the house because everyone is out to get me.' Although Mary's case and Edna Foa's book show that certain conditions militate against success with behavioural therapy these cases are rare in my experience.

The agoraphobic patient who literally cried for help

In addition to avoiding buses, patients with agoraphobia usually also avoid aeroplane and train travel which severely limits their holiday options. They also avoid lifts, tunnels and any closed-in spaces, as well as the open ones. More rarely, patients feel insecure in their own homes if shut in or at night, but it is most common for home to represent the one safe place they prefer never to leave.

Sometimes the feeling of being shut in can cause a patient to cry out. Barry suffered from attacks of discomfort, fear of fainting and palpitations for fifteen years, and these became so bad that he had to give up his work as a mathematics teacher. He told me that during the attacks, which occurred several times a day, with no obvious cause, he became shaky, could not concentrate, cringed and could not help himself from crying out, 'Help!' He stopped driving his car and later on avoided public transport. In addition Barry had the odd experience of depersonalization: he felt that he was not really there when he had these attacks, and when his feet touched the pavement he had the bizarre feeling of walking on air.

He was a happily married man with two children and no past history of psychiatric illness. His mother had had fears of going out and feared going on buses, and had been treated by her general practitioner with sedative drugs. But the general impression Barry gave was of an easy-going personality and he had many friends. It was difficult to see how an intelligent and otherwise well-adjusted person could be so disabled. The first time I went out with him we travelled on a bus, and after about

five minutes he shouted in a loud voice, *'Help!'* He then said,
'I'm terribly embarrassed about this. I hope you will forgive me.
I just can't stop myself. Here it comes again . . . 'Help!'

Barry had lost his job and could not travel anywhere, either
by car or public transport. His life was ruined by phobic disability, but his cry for help did not go unheeded: he was treated in
research projects at the Maudsley Hospital during the 1970s and
he has remained well to this day. The details of his treatment
will not be given here as they are similar to others described in
this chapter.

Playground panic and the protective husband

'I just can't take the children to school any more, and it
makes me feel so stupid,' explained Jill. She went on to elaborate how seven weeks earlier she had suffered a panic attack in
the playground when taking her two children to school and,
that as she dreaded another attack, she had since stopped
going there. A few weeks later she avoided large shops and
supermarkets. When she had attempted to collect her children
from school again she felt her heart racing and was convinced
that she would pass out. She then arranged for her husband or
friends to collect the children and to do the shopping for her.

'This is so stupid. It's ruining my life. I can't go on depending
on other people like this,' Jill said, tearing her Kleenex into
small pieces in her anxiety. She was by no means a stupid
woman and had worked as a legal secretary for eight years, then
trained as a veterinary nurse. She had married young at the age
of twenty-one, and her two children were three and five. 'I'm
happily married and my husband is very understanding and very
supportive,' was her comment on her marriage. Experience
taught me to ask just what she meant. 'As soon as all this
started, my husband said I was not to put myself through this
agony. He was wonderful. He took the children to school,
collected them, and did all the shopping. One day recently I
thought I might have a go at taking them, but he said I looked a
little pale and persuaded me to stay home. In order to help my

confidence I have gone with him a few times but he takes me straight home if I'm at all anxious.'

Working with Jill and her husband together proved vital at this stage and he took a great deal of convincing that being a caring husband was compatible with helping Jill *face*, not avoid, difficult situations: 'You mean I should take her to the playground and leave her there?'

'You could wait in the car for a while at first, then if she has an overpowering desire to rush out you can comfort her. But can you see how by remaining at her side she never gets the chance to learn to face the situation on her own? You need to prove to both of you that she *can* cope.'

Jill managed to persuade her husband that he was showing care and concern by *not* taking her into the playground, and that he had been unwittingly increasing her avoidance problem. We then devised a strategy to overcome Jill's avoidance. As she most feared the playground and shops when they were crowded, her husband suggested that by taking the children a few minutes earlier than usual, and by choosing the least busy days to shop, she could gradually overcome her anxiety. Jill's husband had become 'very understanding and very supportive' in a different sense.

It took several months of patient treatment for Jill *and* her husband to learn the importance of her gradually learning to face up to the situations she had avoided. But it was worth it as the last time I saw them she told me with a large smile how she was able to take the children to school with little difficulty.

June overcomes agoraphobia with her husband's help

June, a 22-year-old married woman, was brought to the clinic by her husband. She had been married a year and from that time had been unable to go to work as she feared travelling alone. Her husband, a security man, worked shifts and was often out all night. On these occasions June would ask her older, unmarried sister to sleep in the house with her. Once, when her husband had been called out unexpectedly at night, June had a panic attack and had called the general practitioner as she believed she was going to die. Following this episode, they had been referred to the local psychiatric services where they had marital counselling which they found unhelpful.

I discovered that June, the youngest of a family of two girls and three boys, had always been an anxious and shy person. At the age of fourteen, recovering from influenza, she had fainted during morning assembly and had then been unwilling to return to school. After a week at home, she eventually agreed to go back, on condition that her older sister accompanied her to the gates and met up with her at break and lunchtime. She was accompanied on the journey to and from school until she left at sixteen.

June started work as a typist in an insurance office close to where her sister worked, and they always walked to work together. She avoided travelling on buses or trains, frightened that she might faint. Just before her marriage she passed her driving test but didn't drive unaccompanied as she feared fainting at the wheel. Her husband Barry, a childhood sweetheart, believed that her anxiety problems would improve once she was in her own home. Their names had been down on the local authority housing list for two years and they moved into their flat following the wedding. To get to work June now needed to catch either a bus or train. She attempted to go to work on the first day after moving, but panicked at the bus stop and returned home. Since then she had stayed off work.

June's symptoms were explained to her along these lines: 'Although you have always been a shy and nervous person, it seems that your problems really began after you had fainted at school. This was an unpleasant experience, which you learned to associate with being away from your family. Following this, you avoided going anywhere alone and this strengthened your belief. You never allowed yourself to discover whether or not you could be alone without fainting. So, now, whenever you face the prospect of being alone, you take precautions to prevent it. When you went to the bus stop to go to work, you were tense because you expected something dreadful might happen. Because you were tense, you began to notice the physical symptoms of your anxiety. For example, your heart was pounding and you believed that this was evidence that something terrible was about to happen and that you might die.'

The next step was to teach the couple about anxiety: possible physical and emotional symptoms; how avoidance of feared situations led to further avoidance; how during exposure to fear-provoking situations anxiety does eventually reduce, even though this can take up to two hours. Finally they were told that if this exposure exercise was practised regularly, anxiety gradually reduces in both intensity and duration.

To help them remember this information it was summarized as *Three Golden Rules* for exposure treatment:

1 ANXIETY IS UNPLEASANT BUT IT DOES NO HARM I will not die, go mad or lose control
2 ANXIETY DOES EVENTUALLY REDUCE It cannot continue indefinitely if I continue to face up to the situation
3 PRACTICE MAKES PERFECT The more I repeat a particular exposure exercise, the easier it becomes.

It was necessary then to identify the targets of treatment with the patient. June chose five specific tasks that she would like to be able to perform by the end of treatment to demonstrate that she had improved:

1 To drive alone on the motorway to visit an old school friend in Camberley
2 To travel to work alone on the bus during the rush hour
3 To travel to work alone on the train during the rush hour
4 To travel alone by bus and underground train into the centre of London, and to visit the main shopping areas
5 To remain in the flat alone overnight while Barry was on a night shift.

June decided that it would be easiest for her to start by tackling the problem of walking alone. Barry agreed to be involved in the treatment and to act as her co-therapist. Every evening, when Barry returned from work, they were to go out for a walk. June was to leave first on a predetermined route while Barry was to wait for five minutes and then follow in her footsteps. They were to take care that the exposure time was long enough for June's anxiety to reduce, usually between one and two hours. June was to record details of the exposure exercises in her diary and to note also her anxiety levels at the beginning, middle and towards the end of the exposure task. To introduce some consistency into the anxiety ratings, she was asked to use a 0–8 scale where 0 indicated no anxiety and 8 extreme anxiety or panic. If June found that her anxiety levels were reducing during the week, she was to go out for a long walk alone.

At the second session the following week, June and Barry were delighted that not only had June managed to go on a walk alone but she had even gone shopping in the local shops while Barry stayed home. Praised for this excellent progress, it was then suggested to June that the session could be used to start tackling bus travel. She agreed but felt that she would prefer to begin on old-fashioned buses with an open platform rather than on the more difficult driver-only buses with doors which shut. At first June asked if Barry could sit next to her but eventually agreed to sit at the front of the bus, with Barry and the therapist at the back. After a few minutes, June was very anxious and came to complain of symptoms of panic. She was gently reminded that this feeling, although unpleasant, would eventually pass, whereas, if she gave up, her anxiety might be even worse next time. She returned to her seat and after forty-five minutes looked much more relaxed and cheerful. At the prearranged stop, we all left the bus. Praised by both the therapist and her husband, June expressed delight at her achievement and asked to go alone into a nearby supermarket while we waited outside. She was again praised for this decision and managed to buy a trolley of groceries despite crowds in the store.

On the return journey, June sat alone upstairs on the bus while we sat downstairs. Again she coped excellently and readily agreed to continue this practice with Barry during the following week. She was to start using driver-only buses once her confidence increased, and then to tackle bus travel alone.

For the third session it was arranged that the therapist only would meet June outside an underground station as Barry was unable to be there. June travelled to the station alone on a bus and her exposure to underground travel followed a similar pattern to the session with bus travel. The fourth and fifth sessions were held at the outpatient clinic. June and Barry gradually increased the homework exposure and June practised travelling alone to her place of work by bus and train, and was able to return to work before the end of the fifth week. She also travelled up to London alone when Barry was at work. June also began working on her fear of being alone at home overnight. Initially she stayed in the house during the day and evening, and then progressed to being alone overnight when she knew that her sister was at her home. She was surprised and pleased when she did not feel the need to phone her sister and felt able to be alone without taking these precautions. Throughout this time the therapist monitored her progress, praised her success and suggested tasks to attempt.

By session six most of the treatment targets had been achieved, though driving alone had proved difficult. Barry was concerned that she might become very anxious and 'do something silly', and so had been unwilling to encourage her to practise driving. As June found it easier to drive on quiet roads, the therapist and Barry sat in the car while June drove from the clinic into the country. Again, she found this easier than she had anticipated and agreed that, after forty-five minutes of driving, she would stop at a station where the therapist and Barry would catch a train while she drove herself back to the clinic. This demonstration proved to both June and Barry that she was able to drive sensibly and safely. Following this session June continued to practise driving over the next three weeks. Initially she drove on quiet roads and then on increasingly busy roads in town. Driving in lines of traffic when she was in the right-hand lane and felt unable to 'escape' was particularly difficult for her, and so she devised some routes which involved doing this. Her confidence increased as she practised and she then began travelling on motorways at relatively quiet off-peak times, progressing to busier periods. Session seven was used to reiterate the principles of treatment which June had successfully learned and applied. She had achieved all her targets of treatment, and, while congratulating her, the therapist warned that she would still need to continue practising over the following months. Everyone has good and bad days, weeks or months, and it was important for June to continue to face up to difficult situations even during the bad times when she felt more anxious. Any periods of illness which restricted her activities could lead to a slight increase in fear when she returned to her normal activities.

June's case illustrates how a young woman with a moderately severe phobia was treated with the help of her husband and fourteen hours of the therapist's time over a seven-week period. The time varies with individual patients, however, and not everyone has a supportive partner, relatives or friends to help out.

Must I go through this torture every day?

Gillian is a 24-year-old secretary who begins to have anxiety symptoms each day before setting off for work. She dreads going on the underground train and starts to sweat, has pains in her stomach, feels sick and fears she will pass out. When she enters the train she feels these symptoms worsen and then she also experiences palpitations. Although she has had these symptoms since the age of eighteen, she has *never* stayed away from work nor has she avoided travel on the underground train.

The very first attack of anxiety that Gillian remembered was in school assembly at the age of seventeen when she thought that she would pass out. After her first attack, she experienced further palpitations. She had been allowed to avoid school assembly whenever she felt anxious and had done so on numerous occasions.

The explanation in behavioural terms went something like this: avoidance of a feared situation (crowded school assembly) had been learned. This behaviour had generalized to the crowded underground train. At the present time Gillian was regularly facing a feared situation but, as is sometimes the case, the anxiety would not habituate despite regular and long exposure.

The attacks happened like this. When she was standing on the train platform, Gillian would have a bad attack of anxiety, and say to herself: 'This is it. The train will never come. I am going to freak out and collapse. I am breathing too fast and my heart is going too fast. I must give up my job and stop putting myself through this torture every day.'

Gillian was asked to record these thoughts each day on a chart, and in the next session the therapist examined *the evidence* for each thought with her:

THERAPIST: So what makes you think you will freak out and collapse?

PATIENT: I feel this pounding in my chest. It is most unpleasant and I feel I am going to die.

THERAPIST: What is the evidence that you will collapse in an attack?

PATIENT: Well, there isn't any so far, but there is always a first time!

THERAPIST: So the pounding in your chest leads to the thought that you might die, even though you know this is unlikely. If we could think of a way to bring on the attack just by exercise, then perhaps you could see that the extra activity of your heart is a way of your heart providing more blood needed for exercise.

PATIENT: How could I do that?

THERAPIST: If you were to run up and down on the spot and then see if it produces similar symptoms. Could that prove something to you?

(The patient agreed to do this activity for about three minutes and the therapist did it at the same time. They then each measured the other's pulse rate.)

Right, so how do you feel now and what does it tell you?

PATIENT: My heart is pounding in the same way that I worry about. Your pulse is even more rapid than mine after the exercise and yet you look fine. I suppose that exercise brings on the same symptoms. A possible explanation for my symptoms is that I over-react to my normal bodily functioning.

Later in treatment Gillian made cue cards based on her thought diaries and with their regular use she felt somewhat less anxious about going to work. But on a 0 to 8 scale of symptom severity, she scored 8 at the start and 6 at the end of six sessions with no indication that her anxiety would decrease any further. She had previously been treated with a variety of tablets to reduce anxiety but to no effect. Yet she still travelled on the underground train. It is unusual, but not unknown, for patients to have anxiety without avoidance. Gillian was praised for facing the feared situation and the dangers of not doing so were pointed out to her. Learning to *live with fear* is a necessity for some patients, although they can be reassured that as the years go by the intensity of the fear does usually diminish.

All the cases I have described so far fit the clinical description vividly described by Westphal more than a century ago. Sufferers from the milder kinds of phobias will be interested in what they can do to help themselves. The last chapter is for them.

3 Social Phobias

'I'm really a timid person – I was beaten up by
Quakers'

– Woody Allen, *Sleeper*

People with agoraphobia may need self-help because they are
too scared to go out to get the professional help they need.
People with social phobias[1] are the 'really timid people' who,
because of this timidity, may also not be able to get any
professional aid. The American Psychiatric Association has defined social phobia as:

> a persistent fear of one or more situations in which the person
> is exposed to possible scrutiny by others and fears that he or
> she may do something or act in a way that will be embarrass-
> ing. Examples include: being unable to continue talking while
> speaking in public, choking on food when eating in front of
> others, being unable to pass water in a public lavatory, hand-
> trembling when writing in the presence of others, and saying
> foolish things or not being able to answer questions in social
> situations.

Most kinds of phobias are commoner in women than in men
but social phobias reverse this pattern: men were in the majority
(77 per cent) among cases in a study of patients selected for
social skills training. Most socially phobic patients suffer in
crowded restaurants, and some are even afraid to go out to
dinner or to invite others to meals with them at home. They will
often be frightened to write in public and, in particular, avoid
writing a cheque or handling money in front of others in case
their hand shakes. With many patients their fear is worse in
front of the opposite sex, although there are usually no specific
sexual problems.

As with agoraphobia, these social fears lead to avoidance which has profound implications on life-style. Sufferers avoid talking or eating in public, walking past bus queues, sitting opposite others on a train or a bus, going to parties or to a public swimming-pool. Patients will use alcohol or minor tranquillizers to help them cope with social situations, risking dependency on these substances.

A common underlying fear these patients have is that they are blushing and that people are looking at them. This fear increases their anxiety so any blushing becomes worse. They may also fear that their hands will shake, for example, when performing an insignificant action such as drinking a cup of tea, and this *fear* of trembling is usually totally out of proportion to the actual minor tremor. Sufferers may also have an underlying fear of vomiting, without ever having actually done so. This fear may be made worse if they are in the presence of others who could vomit. This has led one patient to avoid public houses or to being with young children.

A young man socially disabled by phobia

Jeffrey was hiding behind a newspaper in the waiting-room and when called for his appointment did not look up but kept his eyes firmly fixed on the floor. During the interview he did not look at the therapist and his voice was barely audible. In muted tones he described how he had been shy from his schooldays, despite a close and warm relationship with his parents. At university his shyness had prevented him joining in social activities and he spent his holidays with his parents or other family members.

He had trained as a librarian and enjoyed his job except when it brought him into contact with the public. His extreme shyness had been noticed and was threatening to hold up promotion. He always ate sandwiches alone to avoid joining colleagues, and his social life was so poor he had become a virtual recluse. His main spare-time activities were watching television alone or playing chess with a computer. The most fearful situation for Jeffrey was talking to a young woman when he would become lost for words and feared blushing. He had a poor opinion of himself and thought that he would fail even before he tried. This expectation of failure had become self-fulfilling and was why he never met young women. He now totally avoided feared situations and felt even more badly about himself.

The therapist started by asking Jeffrey in what ways he thought his behaviour ought to be changed: 'Tell me, Jeffrey, what would you like to do that you find too difficult or painful at the moment?'

He responded initially with three suggestions:

I suppose I ought to be able to look you in the face.
Then I'd like to be able to talk to people without blushing.
I would like to be able to eat in front of other people especially at work.

And, finally, he admitted in a whisper, 'It would be great if I could chat to women like other blokes do.' These four statements were taken as behavioural targets for us to work at in therapy.

The problem of his gaze aversion was dealt with by guidance and demonstration. Firstly, a co-therapist and the therapist demonstrated how they looked at each other during a conversation and Jeffrey was asked to watch. When the therapist asked him to copy the behaviour he reverted to his habitual gaze aversion. He was then given direct training in looking the therapist in the face. Therapist: 'I am going to look *you* in the face and I want you to stare directly back at me. No matter how hard this is, do not look away.' After staring at each other for two minutes, the therapist asked Jeffrey how he felt and he said, 'Most uncomfortable. I wish the earth would open and swallow me up. I feel hot and red, and very embarrassed.' Despite these feelings, it was possible to encourage Jeffrey to look directly at the therapist for very brief periods. The time spent looking was slowly increased until he could tolerate five seconds. The time continued being gradually increased, first of all with the therapist speaking while Jeffrey listened, and finally Jeffrey spoke while the therapist listened. At the end of six sessions along these lines Jeffrey no longer felt hot and uncomfortable.

This deliberate staring was a method used to encourage direct exposure to the feared situation. Staring itself is not usually socially appropriate and so some time was then spent discussing with the patient the *rules of eye contact*. Brief contact with the eyes is made on first meeting someone and then it is useful to make brief eye contact again when making a point, but direct eye contact is broken and intermittent during normal conversation. It is also usual to make brief eye contact on parting. After repeated practice Jeffrey gradually became less worried about looking the therapist in the eye for prolonged periods and he was given homework tasks to look at other people, such as his landlady, while engaging them in conversation, obeying the rules of eye contact.

We next made a videotape of an interview between Jeffrey and a friendly female medical student. The student was a socially skilled attractive young woman who asked Jeffrey all about his work in the library. When the videotape was played back he was seen to make good eye contact and was praised for this. In general, it is best to begin by emphasizing *positive* behaviour before going on to negative criticism. It was immediately clear that Jeffrey's conversational skills were poor as he never initiated discussion and spoke in a soft, barely audible voice. He was completely inaudible on the videotape feedback and attention was now focused on his voice production. He had already been given *positive* feedback on what he was doing well, such as his improved posture. After each of the following had been demonstrated to him he was encouraged to practise:

1 Using an expressive tone
2 Speaking fluently
3 Speaking faster
4 Using authoritative and powerful language.

He carried a card into the next session with these instructions written on it. He soon began to use more appropriate intonation, but had to guard against too high a pitch. His fluency also improved with practise, especially when he had formulated his thoughts in advance. As his confidence increased, he was able to speak faster and more powerfully. It was suggested that he avoid prefatory remarks such as I think, I guess and I mean, and stop expressing *uncertainty* with statements that sounded like questions. Whenever he used an expressive tone, spoke fluently and faster, or more powerfully, his achievement was praised.

One social situation that Jeffrey particularly feared was his weekly visit to the launderette: 'I dread having to speak to someone so I usually take a book.' The therapist suggested: 'Leave the book behind and start a conversation with a young woman along the lines of: "Could you show me how to work this machine?"' This was very successful as the particular young woman had then talked in a non-threatening way about the neighbourhood and Jeffrey was able to practise his newfound voice production and conversational skills.

In some cases therapy is not as straightforward as this and, if difficulties are encountered, more complicated techniques can be used. One such is role-play and role-reversal. The patient plays someone he fears encountering, such as the young woman, and the therapist could take the role of Jeffrey himself. The therapist would act as a competent model and the patient would be exposed to a useful learning situation. At the next stage, the patient 'plays' himself and the therapist plays the young woman.

A further refinement is to use an ear-microphone so that when the patient is totally lost for words he can be prompted by the therapist watching the session through a one-way screen. For the patient who becomes speechless in certain situations a script can also be a useful tool. It can be written as a homework exercise and then be discussed and edited. Reading from the script in practice sessions is gradually phased out for real-life practice.

A childhood experience that had to be faced

The next case is one of those in which the patient's understanding of her symptoms involved re-experiencing the original situation.

Dora, a 25-year-old married woman, had found difficulty

eating in public all her life. She completed the exposure therapy exercises to her avoided situations but, despite overcoming avoidance, she still felt very anxious whenever she had to eat with someone looking at her.

I explained: 'Sometimes you have an image in your mind which leads you to become anxious in a situation. If we can run through this image, rather like playing back a film, it might help. Please close your eyes and imagine you are sitting at a table with a plate of food in front of you. How does that make you feel?'

Dora replied, 'I feel anxious. It is a horrible feeling. My stomach is contracting and I can feel waves of panic passing over me.'

I now tried to find out how she had felt when it first started by asking, 'You have told me that you have had this symptom since childhood. Can you try to recall when it first started and how you felt at that time?'

Dora was silent for a few moments, then said, 'I was a child at school. We were having school dinners and I can remember this dinner lady standing over me. She insisted that I finished all the food on my plate and this made me very anxious because I knew I could not.'

I then asked, 'Now tell me what is happening and what you are feeling.'

Dora's face flushed and she replied in a loud voice, 'I am angry with that dinner lady.'

I asked, 'Why do you think you are angry?'

She looked thoughtful and said, 'I am sure it is because of her that I have problems now. But I can't get back at her after all these years . . . She may not even be alive.'

I then attempted to explore her own idea about her anger by saying, 'You are right, you cannot get back at her. However, we have an idea here that your pent-up anger might still be causing you problems. Can we test this out in some way?'

She responded, 'Get the anger out, you mean? Then, if I feel better, it may have proved something?'

I suggested a method for her to get rid of her anger. 'Yes, and one way to do this is to imagine the dinner lady is really sitting here with us in this room, and you give her a piece of your mind. Could you try that now?'

Dora shouted out loudly, 'You bossy, power-crazed bitch, why don't you pick on someone your own size instead of pushing little children around? ... In your position of authority you ought to understand how difficult it is for children to eat in a hurry ... They only have small stomachs, you know, and if you make a child anxious it makes it even worse ... If I could get hold of you, I would teach you a lesson you won't forget ...'

As a homework exercise Dora was asked to write an essay entitled 'Instructions to Dinner Ladies', to put her feelings on paper as a way of further playing out the imagery and reliving the emotional experience. Further sessions were spent reviewing the homework and encouraging expression of anger. The use of imagery here produced a good and lasting result, whereas the standard therapy alone was inadequate. Dora had remained without symptoms when she came to see me for a follow-up session a year later.

The girl who blushed to stop blushing

Viktor Frankl published articles on paradoxical intention drawing on his harrowing experiences in Nazi concentration camps.[2] He maintained that every individual has to find a meaning in his or her life to overcome suffering and neurotic disability. He also pointed out: 'A phobic person usually tries to avoid the situation in which anxiety arises ... and the result is a strengthening of the symptom. Conversely, if we succeed in bringing the patient to the point where he ceases to flee from or fight his symptoms, but on the contrary even exaggerates them, then we may observe that the symptoms diminish and that the patient is no longer haunted by them.'

Paradoxical intention is a bizarre treatment on first consideration: if someone has a problem you tell them to make it worse! However, in neurotic disorders, it can be the very act of trying to get better that makes you worse. For sexual difficulties where a couple have been trying hard to succeed at intercourse and repeatedly failing, in paradoxical intention they are told:

'Whatever you do, do *not* attempt intercourse for the next two weeks.' Time and again, I have been told by such patients when they return after the prescribed period: 'We tried hard to comply with your instructions, Doctor, but we do not know how it happened, we just had to give in, and amazingly the problem went away.'

Another condition where paradoxical intention has been used is for sleep disturbance. The fear of sleeplessness increases sleep disturbance because anticipation that you will not sleep makes you anxious and prevents sleep. Dubois, the famous French psychiatrist (cited by Frankl), compared sleep to a dove which has landed near one's hand and stays there as long as no attention is paid to it. If you try to take hold of it, it flies away. Accordingly, Frankl advised his patient to stay awake as long as possible. In this way, the anticipatory anxiety of not being able to fall asleep was replaced by the paradoxical intention of not falling asleep at all. Frankl reported that his patient was soon able to go to sleep normally.

Frankl also described how he treated a patient with a fear of blushing by asking him to try to blush as much as possible. This man feared blushing so much that he actually did blush as soon as he feared he would. This anticipation of fear, known as anticipatory anxiety, is one common to many phobias, as I have mentioned. Asking him to blush took away his anticipation of anxiety because the blushing was then under his control.

A further aspect of paradoxical intention emphasized by Frankl is the use of humour. He would often try to get his patients to see the funny side of their symptoms and, by laughing at themselves, reduce some of the anxiety. Humour helps people look at themselves and their problem in a more detached way. It appears to be a quality unique to humans for, as far as we know, no animal laughs at itself.

A final point about paradoxical intention, in line with many behavioural treatments, is that it puts the emphasis on the patient to change his attitude towards his fear, and so cure him or herself rather than develop a dependency on the therapist.

Many people blush but some find this symptom dominates their lives to such an extent that they seek medical help. Connie was an attractive young woman of twenty-five, who described her difficulties with blushing: 'Whenever I sense that people are looking at me, I come over all hot. I can feel the heat radiating off my cheeks and face, neck and the upper part of my body, and I always wear dresses or blouses with high necks and collars. Going swimming is completely out of the question.'

Connie's early childhood was unremarkable, as was her career as a successful secretary. She had a happy relationship with her boyfriend and they had plans to marry. He was somewhat amused by her problem and failed to see why she was so concerned about it. He had never felt any desire to visit elegant restaurants where Connie would have liked to wear low-cut dresses.

What explanation could be given to help Connie with the problem *she* considered serious despite her boyfriend's attitude? What seemed to bring on her blushes was if she felt people were looking at her when the top part of her body was exposed. She would also blush if someone in the office called out her name in a loud voice.

One theory about blushing is that some people have blood vessels in the face which tend to expand and contract more readily than most other people's. This is called labile blood flow. Blushing may be an autonomic response specifically linked to certain social cues and blushers become phobic in these situations. I explained this to Connie and her boyfriend and, despite his apparent casualness about her problem, he then made a suggestion to help Connie confront her problem in a very direct way: 'How about if you look at yourself in a mirror naked from the waist up, and I call out your name in a loud voice?' Connie blushed deeply in the consulting-room when he said this and then she burst into a laugh. 'I really think this is so funny . . . I come here to stop blushing and here I am doing it . . . I just can't take this seriously!'

I pointed out that not taking herself so seriously could be an important part of her treatment. I then asked her to do the same exercise at home with her boyfriend and if they both had a good laugh while she was trying to blush this would be no bad thing. She said, 'What! Stand there starkers in front of a mirror while he calls out my name? I'll either die of embarrassment or die laughing!' However, after a little further thought she agreed to try the experiment on a daily basis and keep a record of her anxiety and the extent of the blushing on each occasion. I was not at all sure if she would be able to do this but considered it worth trying.

At the next session they reported that something quite remarkable had happened. When Connie had stood naked in front of the mirror and her boyfriend had called out her name she had been *unable* to blush. Because she could not blush in a situation where she was certain she would, she thought she would *try* as hard as possible to bring on a blushing attack. But nothing happened. She then thought she might use this method in her office. It worked: as long as she tried hard to blush she was unable to. Connie had discovered for herself the efficacy of paradoxical intention.

4 Animal Phobias

Spider phobia

I was told to go to the basement of an old Victorian house owned by the Institute of Psychiatry in London. I was a young trainee psychiatrist and my guide a more senior trainee called George. I had a long-standing interest in phobias and there was talk at the Institute that some new and exciting research in this field was going on in this basement. I was to carry out a small research project and write it up to complete my training.

'So what actually happens here?' I asked George.

'Watch out for that step! People usually trip up on it.'

We entered a rather dark corridor down some steps to the side of the house which I imagined once would have led to a cellar.

'It all happens down here,' George said in a friendly way.

It smelt a bit damp with a slight odour of gas, and the doors to rooms off the corridor were painted bright orange. We stopped outside a door different from the others in that it was covered with the kind of polystyrene tiles used for sound insulation.

'So we can't hear the patients screaming from outside!' George joked. I *hoped* he was joking. On the door was written:

NO ENTRY
POLYGRAPHIC RECORDING IN PROGRESS
KEEP OUT

George opened the door and motioned with one hand for me to enter and with the other put a finger to his lips forbidding me the questions I was bursting to ask. Inside the sound-proofed room the only chair was taken by a man sitting at a bank of illuminated dials, wearing headphones. He was the polygraph technician and reminded me of cinema images of Second World War submarine echo-detector operators: scruffy, with a beard, old jeans and a sweater with holes. He looked vaguely annoyed by our presence but concentrated on listening to his headphones which conveyed the sound from an adjoining room where a senior psychiatrist was carrying out a treatment session with a patient suffering from spider phobia. I could see what was going on but I could not hear anything from the treatment room. The technician was watching the polygraph doing its work of recording on moving paper the physiological responses of the patient. Its pens scuttled on the paper and I could recognize one channel which appeared to be an ECG. The other channels were measuring skin resistance, a measure of how the body responds to stress. The technician made a few adjustments to the dials on the machine, took off the headphones and indicated for me to wear them.

Now I could see *and* hear what was going on in the treatment room. The patient was a young man in a leather jacket, with wires coming from his sleeves, sitting in a large expensive-looking padded armchair. These wires seemed to join up at the floor and passed through a large plastic tube to the polygraph room. There was a small table with a glass jam jar containing a small spider in front of the young man. The psychiatrist sitting opposite the patient said: 'This is probably going to be very hard for you to do the first time but remember how once you thought it would be quite impossible?'

'You're telling me, Doc!'

The young man with a spider phobia was being encouraged by the doctor to do the very thing he was most scared of: touch the spider. According to theory, even *thinking* about touching something a phobic patient fears will bring on anxiety. The psychiatrist said: 'I want you first of all to sit back in your chair and just think about touching the spider.'

I looked down at the polygraphic recording and the pens made violent up and down oscillations that seemed to take them off the edge of the recording paper. George gave me a thumbs-up sign which I took to mean that this was supposed to happen and the technician adjusted his dials to prevent excessive movement of the pens. After a few minutes the physiological recording settled back to normal.

The psychiatrist then said: 'And now what do you think the next step should be?'

The young man shrugged. 'I suppose you want me to touch the damned thing . . . Do you realize what you are asking here? This is very hard . . . I feel terrible.'

'You know from our previous sessions that you are not compelled to do anything here. You can stop the therapy any time you want. Just tell me and I will take off the measuring instruments and end the session. But if you want to continue with your excellent progress so far, you will try as hard as you can to touch the spider now.'

He reached out and touched it with one finger. Then he immediately withdrew his finger. 'There! I've done it. Ugh!'

'Well done! Do you think you could try to hold your hand there now for five minutes or so?'

'You are asking a great deal, Doc. But if you think it's important I'll try.'

The patient put his hand on the jam jar and held it there while the polygraph pens danced up and down vigorously. The psychiatrist praised the patient and eventually he was able to keep touching the jam jar and it seemed to me that the polygraph showed less extreme responses as time went by. Then the patient was disconnected from the recording electrodes, the psychiatrist shook his hand and made an appointment to see him the following week.

George later gave me the background to this case: 'His name is Bill and, as I recall, he has always disliked spiders. He said that as a child he would run in from the garden crying if he saw a spider there. But he only presented for treatment of his spider phobia at the age of seventeen. When I first met him, he looked the least likely candidate for an anxiety disorder of any kind: he was a large man of over six foot, wearing motor cyclist's gear. He told me of his long-standing fear of spiders and how it prevented him putting his motor cycle away in the garden shed. Although it was his pride and joy, he had to leave his motor cycle in front of his house. This case illustrates the very discreet nature of the specific phobic's disability, as well as the feature common to all the phobias: avoidance.'

'How do phobias like this start?'

'In many adults the origins are not as clear as they are in Bill's case. In children, the common animal fears subside without any apparent reason or sometimes because the patient has been exposed to gradual relearning situations. It isn't known why a small percentage continue after puberty.'

As George enlightened me, several other psychiatrists then joined our discussion over coffee. One said, 'I think this behavioural therapy is dangerous stuff. How do you know that you will not push your patient over the edge? How do you know you won't make Bill psychotic?' George replied by saying that it was most unlikely but of course all new treatments carried risks. (With the hindsight of modern developments we now know that patients do not become psychotic with behavioural therapy nor do they develop other symptoms.)

Someone else said, 'The trouble with this treatment is not that it makes patients mad but that it is just so slow that it bores the therapist to death!' There was silence at the table.

Then someone suggested an approach to speed things up. 'There is a theory in psychology called overlearning. This means that to teach a response that will last and be quickly effective you need to use a very large stimulus. Why don't you try using a bird-eating spider?' Most of us thought that this was a crazy suggestion until we discovered that we would not have to use a live bird-eating spider. It seems that these animals slough their skin on a regular basis and that the skin is an exact replica of the living animal. Someone had a friend at the spider house at London Zoo and all that was needed was for us to collect a bird-eating spider skin from him.

At the next treatment session Bill was asked how he felt about having a large bird-eating spider, albeit a dead one, on the table in front of him and, to our surprise, he agreed to it. The therapist discovered that if a pencil was manoeuvred under the spider, it could be made to move in a most realistic fashion and Bill's polygraph recordings proved that this produced a marked physiological reaction. This strong reaction proved extremely effective and, in about six more sessions, Bill was cured of his spider phobia. He remained cured when I saw him two years later and told me with great satisfaction how he could put his motor cycle away in the garden shed: 'After seeing that bird-eating monster, little garden spiders don't bother me any more!'

A simple snake phobia

Nowadays treatment for animal phobias with behavioural therapy is routine and accepted, but patients still present treatment challenges. Staff at my clinic thought it was a bit of a joke when I wrote in my appointment diary opposite a patient's name REMEMBER TO BRING PLASTIC SNAKE. But it was no joke for Laura, the patient concerned, who was scared to leave her house for fear that she saw a snake in any form. She avoided walking along roads in case she saw an advertisement with a snake in it and she would not use public transport for the same reason. She refused to travel abroad, with the one exception of New Zealand which has no snakes.

I had bought the cheap plastic snake with my young son, who advised me on the choice of colour and length, in a local toy shop. It was about three feet long, black and white, with realistic simulations of scale markings, a red-painted protruding tongue and the words MADE IN TAIWAN on the underside. At the assessment interview Laura had agreed that I could bring the snake to the next session on the strict condition that it remained in my briefcase on the bookcase behind my desk.

'Where is it?' was the first thing she said.

'Exactly where we said it would be.' (I realized that she knew this as she was staring at the briefcase behind my head.)

'So where should we begin?' I asked.

'I want to move my chair nearer the door.'

'Fine. But where should we begin?' I persisted. 'How about letting me get the snake out of the briefcase?'

'I don't think I would like that,' she replied, edging further towards the door.

'I know you won't *like* it but to gain anything from this session you need to try to get used to this plastic snake. Remember it is only plastic.'

'OK . . . I will allow you to get it out . . . but don't let me see it just yet ... Put it behind your briefcase out of view on the table over there.' (She indicated a table about ten feet away.) Laura looked terrified, yet did allow me over about thirty minutes to reveal the plastic snake fully. Why did it so terrify her? Did she think it was a real snake? And how could we progress from this point?

Phobias are irrational, so appeals to logic are of no avail. The discussion on the question of its *reality* led to a reference to the famous painting by Magritte of a pipe entitled 'Ceci n'est ce pas un pipe' (this is not a pipe). Laura, an intelligent and well-educated person, understood the point of Magritte's painting: a representation of something is not the same as the thing itself, but it may bring about a similar *emotional* reaction. Magritte's painted pipe could not be smoked. The plastic snake could not hurt her but it still terrified her. At this stage Laura was reasonably happy looking at the snake, but we both knew she had to touch it to make progress.

'I don't think I'll ever be able to touch it.'

Then I reminded her, 'You didn't think you would ever be able to look at it!'

'I know I've got to do it.'

With coaxing along these lines, Laura eventually agreed to touch the tail of the snake, but immediately gave a shout and pulled away her hand.

I then asked her to go through the rules about dealing with anxiety, and she said, 'Anxiety does no harm, eventually it goes away. The trouble is the anxiety is *not* going away!'

'That is because you are not giving it a chance to go away. You pulled away your hand immediately. Try to hold it there as long as you can.'

Laura then touched the snake and remarked, 'It is pulsating. I swear it is!'

Then we had a discussion of how it was not the snake, of course, but Laura herself who was pulsating and her heightened anxiety exaggerated it. She had had a similar misperception when she thought the snake had moved: she herself had moved it by touching it and her own heightened awareness had led her to jump to the wrong conclusion. After doing so, she wiped her finger repeatedly on her clothing and I asked why she did this.

'It's the Lady Macbeth thing, I suppose. Because I have touched it, I feel bad. I would like to wipe away all contact with it . . . Sounds crazy, doesn't it?'

'No, not crazy at all,' I reassured her. 'But can you guess what I want you to do about it?'

'Sure. Touch it with no wiping. I'll try that now.'

By the end of this session Laura was touching the snake with one finger and was able to keep her finger there. We agreed to meet again in a week.

At the start of the second session Laura seemed to have made no progress. She entered the consulting-room in a state of great anxiety: 'Where is it?'

'The same place as last time. In my briefcase. Do you think you could allow me to put the plastic snake directly on the table now?'

She agreed.

'When you feel comfortable about doing it, can you gradually move your chair a little closer, please?'

'I'll never bloody well feel comfortable about it, but I'm going to try just the same.' In this way she gradually edged her chair closer. Within ten minutes she was touching the snake in the same way that it had taken an hour to achieve in the first session.

I reassured her. 'So you *are* making progress.'

'But how many hours will it take to cure me? At this rate I'll be coming here for years!'

'The rate of progress and the ultimate number of sessions you will need depends on how much you push yourself in each session.'

Laura looked thoughtful and said, 'I have got to get over this bloody phobia. It's so stupid and it's ruining my life. I am going to touch one of the coils *now*!' And, with a muted scream, she grabbed the snake by its tail.

'Well done! Now you are *really* making progress!' In this way, with much encouragement, she ended the second session able to hold on to the snake with both hands and to touch it anywhere, including its head. We discussed where to go from here: it was one thing for her to touch the snake in the consulting-room but quite another for her to touch one outside it. Could she overcome this one? Her idea was to buy her own plastic snake and bring it to the next session. She amazed herself by being able to do this without much difficulty.

Now we had to work out a way to help Laura with her problem of seeing *pictures* of snakes. She said that in some way this would be harder than getting used to the plastic models. I remembered that she would not open magazines or books with pictures for fear she might stumble upon a snake image. I asked her if she would allow me to bring a picture of a snake to the next session.

'OK . . . but make sure I don't see it till I feel ready.'

At home I searched for some snake pictures and among a small collection of books by famous photographers I found a photograph by Helmut Newton entitled 'Woman with snake, Berlin 1979'. What worried me about using this picture was that, as with most of Helmut Newton's work, it was sexually suggestive. The attractive woman was posed to reveal her brassière and, as she stretched her hand out, she gave the impression of holding a large snake between her thumb and forefinger, smiling as she did so. I was not at all sure what Laura would make of it, and I would have chosen a more straightforward, natural history type of picture if I had had the time.

At the session I explained to Laura about the book of photographs I had brought along, and she said: 'Oh, yes, I like Helmut Newton's photographs, especially the way he makes his models appear as real people. Just be careful to hold the book on the other side of the room when you open it at the snake picture!'

My fears of using a book with sexual *and* snake imagery proved groundless. My psychiatric training had conditioned me to assume that any phobia to do with snakes must conceal sexual anxiety about the penis. Laura's case was a good refutation of such simplistic notions: she had a normal sex life with a regular partner and it was only snakes and not penises she was afraid of. In her case, at least, these did not appear to be connected.

She continued in the therapy to approach the photograph of

the snake and within twenty minutes she was able to touch it. After this session, seeing pictures of snakes held no difficulty, and when she left she told me that she had planned a holiday abroad – *not* to New Zealand!

A not so simple snake phobia

Sally began with a plea. 'You won't make me touch any of them, will you?'

'No one is going to make you do anything without your agreement,' I said.

'You are absolutely sure about that?'

'Absolutely.'

She certainly looked in a state of great anxiety: she could hardly sit still in her chair, her hands trembled and her dry mouth prevented her talking until she had drunk a glass of water. Then she said that three months earlier her sister had told her of how she had been sexually abused by their father in childhood. This had involved Satanic rituals with live snakes being draped across her sister's naked body. Since Sally had learnt this, she had been unable to cope with any images of snakes, all of which produced panic attacks. These attacks could also be caused by garden worms and she avoided going into her garden, especially after rain. If someone used the word snake in conversation, it was enough to bring on an attack, and it was soon clear that her anxiety was being increased by my questions about snakes and worms.

In order to test out this idea, I asked Sally for some background information and she appeared less tense as she described her early childhood. She was successful at school, trained as a school teacher, and now was much enjoying her work with children. She was happily married and had no sexual difficulties. Her husband was a policeman and they had a grown-up son at university.

When her symptoms began she went to her general practitioner who prescribed antidepressant medication. 'No use whatsoever, but then I wasn't depressed, was I?' was Sally's comment. She was then referred to a psychologist and given relaxation therapy which made her *worse*: 'When I was asked to take a deep breath and let everything go, the snake pictures in my head became unbearable.' Sally was recounting a well-known complication of relaxation therapy for some patients: they experience a loss of control during the sessions during which intrusive images of the fears become intense. They were so intense in Sally's case it was *as if* she were experiencing the real thing. In psychiatric jargon we call these experiences pseudo-hallucinations and, unlike some kinds of genuine hallucination, they do not indicate a psychotic illness. Nevertheless Sally's pseudo-hallucinations were most unpleasant and enough to put her off relaxation therapy and the psychologist who administered it.

As Sally talked about her problems I tried to understand why they should have started so recently, only after her sister had told her of her sexual abuse in childhood. Had Sally herself been abused by her father? Freud's explanations of phobic neurosis involved the idea of repressed sexual longings about a parent but Sally was more likely to be repressing painful memories of childhood exploitation, although even this was not certain. What *was* certain was that I had agreed with Sally *not* to do anything she did not agree to, and what she did not want was to discuss her father.

The session then focused on behavioural treatment possibilities.

THERAPIST: How do your symptoms come out at work?

SALLY: I manage OK in front of the children.

THERAPIST: Even if they draw pictures of snakes?

SALLY: Yes ... sort of ... I tell them to take the drawing away as I don't like it ... But I never have a panic attack in front of them. The other teachers all know about my problem and they wouldn't use the word or show me any pictures of snakes.

THERAPIST: When the children make models of snakes from clay or plasticine, what happens then?

SALLY: That is not as bad as a picture in a book. I just don't know why. It's irrational.

(The treatment session that followed used a cartoon book of snakes that the patient had brought.)

SALLY: My husband got these cartoon drawings of snakes from the library for me, but of course I haven't looked at them. I thought that cartoon drawings wouldn't be as bad as realistic ones or photographs, but now I'm not so sure that I can even cope with these.

THERAPIST: I would like you to get the book out of your bag and hand it to me, please.

(She did this *very* gingerly, averting her gaze from the well-wrapped book.)

SALLY: You are not going to give me that flooding treatment, Doctor, are you? I've heard about that!

THERAPIST: What we do will be agreed between us before we do it and I am not going to spring anything on you. How about if I get the book out of its wrapper and put it on my lap?

SALLY: OK . . . Just make sure it doesn't fall off on to me!

(I carefully put the book with a cartoon picture of a snake on the cover on my lap.)

SALLY That's terrible! I'm dying here! Something about the head on that thing. It's so *big*. I don't think I can go through with this.

(She looked very distraught at this point, put her hand over her mouth and rapidly shifted her feet up and down. This state of high anxiety only lasted a few minutes, after which she smiled.)

You are more of a bully than my husband.

THERAPIST: I am glad you are smiling now. You have done very well. You see, anxiety really does get less with time. What if I put the picture on the armrest of your chair, but hold it so it could not fall on you?

SALLY: I suppose I have to say yes. Right?

THERAPIST: No, you can stop the treatment any time you want. But I remember how you were at pains to point out that having this phobia is no joke. How you cannot leave your house after it has rained in case there are worms on the path, how you cannot walk down the street because of posters which might have snakes on them . . .

SALLY: I'm surprised at how much hard work this all is. I feel exhausted. But I *must* get over it. Put the thing on my armrest!

(Her anxiety levels shot up as before, but, as before, they came down again in a matter of minutes. She smiled and chatted about how much easier it was for her now to cope with the work. We talked about her fears and their irrationality.)

SALLY: When I looked at that picture, it was as if it was a real snake. For me it *was* a real snake. The trouble is, my imagination works overtime. For instance I can be driving my car and I suddenly get this idea that snakes could appear from under the dashboard. Now I *know* that is crazy! I can get scared at home and persuade myself that snakes could crawl underneath the crack in the door and get me. Now I *know* that is irrational!

THERAPIST: Yes, you are right. It is possible to scare yourself in this way and to make things worse. What we are doing here in this session is the opposite: instead of *imagining* pictures of snakes in your head, you are looking at real pictures until you get used to them. Each time you get used to them here makes it easier in real life.

SALLY: Now I understand why it is important to keep looking at the picture rather than just glimpse it out of the corner of my eye. If I stare at it long and hard enough, the state of shock leaves me and I calm down eventually.

Two weeks later I asked her if I could make a plasticine model of a snake in the treatment room and she agreed. This tentative treatment plan began with small sausage-shaped pieces which later became more snakelike when Sally added eyes in a contrasting colour to the body. We progressed, following a similar procedure to the one we had used with the cartoon book of snakes, and eventually Sally was able to look at colour photographs of snakes in books and magazines, and at realistic plastic models. The day Sally brought in a jar of worms she had herself picked up from her garden after a rainstorm was one to remember.

Dog phobia

The patient was an 18-year-old student teacher who, since childhood, had avoided situations where she might come into contact with dogs. Her family protected her in this way and someone always had to check the garden to ensure that no dogs had strayed there. She crossed the road to avoid dogs and never went into public parks. An interesting point was that her mother remembered that, when she was two years old, she had been frightened by a large dog jumping on to her pram but the patient herself had no recollection of this.

In her first treatment session the patient eventually agreed to stay in the same room with a small dog if it was never closer to her than twelve feet, and then only if it was on a leash. The therapist sat on a chair close to the dog and petted and stroked it while talking to the patient. After about twenty minutes, she approached the dog and was able to imitate the therapist by stroking the dog's back, but she could not be persuaded to touch its head. She would not touch it at all unless it was kept on the leash. After this session the therapist returned to the waiting-room where the patient's aunt said, 'She will *never* agree to having a dog in the same room.' Then the patient told her what had happened in the treatment session.

Four more sessions followed with the emphasis on modelling to make exposure to the dog easier. The therapist modelled touching the dog's head and even put his hand into the dog's mouth. Eventually the patient was able to do this too, even when the dog was unleashed. There were also homework exercises in which she had to visit a friend with a large dog. By the end of treatment she could be alone with the dog in her friend's living room. One year later she was able to visit public parks and had no fear of encountering dogs off the leash.

The successful treatment of spider, snake and dog phobias have been described. Just as good results can be achieved in the treatment of other animal phobias such as cat, bird, frog, moth, bee and wasp phobias. Such phobias all show clear avoidance of these animals. Specific animal phobias are quite distinct from agoraphobia and social phobia as they cause a more localized problem, are associated with only a few other psychiatric symptoms, generally start in early childhood (even though treatment may follow only in adult life) and they run a steady rather than a fluctuating course.

Mild fears of animals are very common but such fears are rarely strong enough to be called a phobia or to bring the patient for therapy. Psychiatrists see far fewer adults with animal phobias than they do those with agoraphobia and social phobias. More animal phobias are found in young children than in adults and most of these get better before puberty.

5 Various Phobias

'The worst thing in the world,' said O'Brien, 'varies from individual to individual. It may be burial alive, or death by fire, or by drowning, or by impalement, or fifty other deaths. There are cases where it is some quite trivial thing, not even fatal.'

– George Orwell,
Nineteen Eighty-four

Samuel Johnson was said to be 'sick of life and afraid of death, and had deep troubles of mind' yet he went on to write the first English dictionary, among other great achievements. This chapter shows that the variety of human fear is as great as life itself and most readers will be able to identify with some aspects of fear. Bizarre and disturbing case histories follow: illness phobia, fear of farting, fear of flying, hospital phobia and others.

Though many patients believe that their phobia is unique, doctors have long realized that most phobias can be categorized into a fairly limited list. Dr Benjamin Rush, one of the signatories of the American Declaration of Independence in 1776, had his own classification:[1]

1 Cat phobia
2 Rat phobia
3 Insect phobia
4 Odor phobia
5 Dirt phobia
6 Rum phobia ('a very rare distemper ... If it were possible to communicate this distemper as we do the small-pox, by inoculation, what an immense revenue would be derived from it by physicians.')
7 Water phobia

8 Solo phobia (fear of being alone)
9 Power phobia
10 Faction phobia (the *opposite* to being afraid of power)
11 The want phobia ('confined chiefly to old people')
12 Doctor phobia
13 Blood phobia
14 Thunder phobia
15 Home phobia
16 Church phobia
17 Ghost phobia
18 Death phobia.

Some of the patients I describe would match many of Rush's categories but nowadays his list would not fit into a serious classification of phobias. Instead, we now group the isolated phobias of animals and insects such as snakes, dogs, cats, spiders, frogs, moths, bees and wasps. Another category is that of specific situations not covered by agoraphobia and social phobia. These include the phobia of thunderstorms, flying phobia, death phobia and illness phobia. This modern classification is reflected in the international classification of diseases brought out by the World Health Organization in 1992, known as *The ICD-10*. In all these cases, especially isolated phobias of animals and insects, *mild fears* are very common. Such fears are rarely strong enough to be called a phobia, but I shall give some examples of cases which *were* severe enough for the patient's general practitioner to refer the patient for specialist psychiatric help.

Thunder phobia

Along with phobias of heights, lifts or other enclosed spaces, phobias of thunderstorms and lightning are common. Patients with the latter problems will often not listen to the weather forecast and will avoid going outdoors if it looks overcast or dark, in case a storm should break. The crucial point here is that their fear concerns a naturally occurring phenomenon and if it is artificially induced, the patient is not phobic of it. In my early researches at the Maudsley Hospital I arranged for a BBC sound effects tape to be played to a patient with thunder phobia in a specially equipped room. The loudest amplifiers and the largest loudspeakers were used, and the tape was played for fifteen minutes. When I asked the patient how he felt, he remarked, 'No effect at all, Doc. It was just a recording, wasn't it?'

Some patients have phobias of dental treatment or of injections, which can lead to their avoidance of these when they are necessary. A rarer syndrome is space phobia, described in four patients by Isaac Marks and Paul Bebbington in 1976.[2] Its hallmark was intense fear, evoked by spatial cues, when standing without support close by. It is distinguished from agoraphobia by the disproportion between the great fear of space and the mild fear of public places in the space syndrome. By contrast, the cardinal feature of agoraphobia is a fear not of open spaces, but of public places, although a mild fear of open spaces sometimes occurs. In 1870 a German psychiatrist named Benedikt called agoraphobia *platschwindel*, meaning 'giddiness in open spaces', and he attributed it to a disease of the inner ear.[3]

Disease phobia

The so-called illness phobia is no longer considered to be a true phobia for, although the patients' fear of disease persists despite medical reassurance, their need for this reassurance is closer to an obsessive-compulsive disorder. Nevertheless some cases are similar to phobias and present fascinating problems of diagnosis and therapy.

'Not one day passes without me having the idea about getting some illness or other. For instance, if I have a headache, I'm convinced it's a brain tumour. If I have a cough, I'm sure it's lung cancer, and recently when my bowels were a little upset, I was sure it was cancer. I have had all the tests done, including several brain scans, and the results are always negative. My own doctor refused any more tests, so I went privately, but when I had used up my savings, I had to go back to the NHS. Most recently I had the idea that I was running a temperature, so I started to take my temperature three or four times each day.'

Rosemary is a 35-year-old intelligent woman who, after describing her worries, told me frankly her self-diagnosis: 'I'm a hypochondriac.' She then went on to describe her career as a journalist, interrupted for several years because of time taken off to visit doctors and hospitals. I guessed, correctly, that she had read a great deal about hypochondriasis and I asked her to tell me what she knew.

'It's a kind of preoccupation with the idea that you have a physical illness, even though doctors keep telling you that you have *not*, and all the tests you have done prove negative. I know *really* that I am unlikely to have cancer but I don't feel happy about it until I have just had an X-ray or brain scan. Then I'm only happy for a short while and the fear of having cancer builds up again. In the case of fear of having a fever, I feel great when I have just taken my temperature and it is normal. The trouble is that this reassurance does not last, and so now I'm kind of addicted to taking my temperature and all the other things. But I do not really consider myself to be a suitable case for a psychiatrist. I mean I'm not off my head, and I'm only depressed because of my fears of illness.'

Rosemary went on to describe how she had had two years of psychoanalysis but it had not helped. Antidepressant medication had been no use either. Rosemary's progress was largely through her own efforts and, possibly, in spite of professional assistance. This thoughtful patient had already worked out more than her diagnosis: she understood how the fear of illness led to reassurance-seeking either from doctors and their tests or by taking her own temperature. The problem she was left with was how to stop seeking this reassurance.

ROSEMARY: I can't live with the uncertainty of whether I have an illness or not.

THERAPIST: One thing I can tell you for certain is that you will remain a hypochondriac until you do learn to live with uncertainty.

ROSEMARY: So how can I change behaviour that has been with me all these years?

THERAPIST: How about making an agreement not to visit any

doctors for at least three months? After all, you could hardly get worse and if, at the end of that time, you go back to your usual behaviour not much will have been lost.

ROSEMARY: You mean no visits to doctors at all? And *no* temperature-taking?

In this case nine sessions were given in a group therapy setting in which patients with similar illness phobias reinforced each other for *not* seeking medical attention. Rosemary, along with most of the other patients in her therapy group, reported success in keeping away from doctors. She had disposed of her collection of thermometers, but on *one* occasion had to go next door to borrow a neighbour's.

Patients with this sort of problem are usually reluctant to accept referral to a psychiatrist because they consider that their condition is due to some undiscovered disease, and they then take a great deal of time in primary care settings. But, with the concept of 'stress' recently becoming widely known among the general public, patients are now more likely to accept a course of therapy labelled 'stress management' rather than referral to a psychiatrist. One theory is that the disorder is a learned behaviour in which the patient focuses unduly on a particular symptom, or set of symptoms, and continued medical investigation serves to reinforce this. Rosemary's treatment was carried out in a group setting in the hope that she would see that she was not unique in having this problem, and also because the patients might help one another become less self-centred.

We cannot fully explain the psychology behind preoccupation with illness. One theory suggests that increased autonomic arousal occurs. The autonomic system has to do with control of heart rate, sweating and bowel action, among other things, and this has the effect on a patient of saying: 'There is something odd happening to me ... It must be that I am unwell.' Or the patient focuses attention on some normal variation of physiological function. For example, Rosemary was preoccupied with minor changes in her temperature and became convinced that this represented something serious and would then check her temperature several times each day with a variety of thermometers.

In this context, seeking reassurance from doctors can make the problem worse. The medical profession is coming to realize the appropriateness of Matthew Prior's eighteenth-century dictum: 'Cured yesterday of my disease, I died last night of my physician.'

I am afraid I am losing my memory: just tell me once more it is OK

There is a well-known cause of loss of memory namely dementia, an organic brain disorder, one kind of which is Alzheimer's disease. Psychiatrists are often asked to assess patients to see if they have this condition, and the assessment involves careful testing of short-term memory which is often followed by blood tests and special kinds of X-rays to detect any brain abnormality. A test of the electrical activity of the brain, an EEG, is also often carried out.

Mrs J was convinced she had Alzheimer's disease despite nothing abnormal being detected on clinical testing. She wanted to be reassured that the tests had been done correctly and that there was nothing wrong with the testing equipment that day. This was after I had spent an hour with her and her husband patiently going over the details of the tests.

It then became clear that I was dealing with a case of what the nineteenth-century French psychiatrists described as *folie de doute* (doubting madness). Here patients develop a syndrome of needing constant reassurance but the more this reassurance is given, the more it is needed. When I explained to Mrs J and her husband that she did not have Alzheimer's disease, my reassurance hardly lasted until she arrived home. Then her husband would telephone me with some complicated questions: 'That EEG machine used to test my wife at St X Hospital. Are you sure that it is as good as at St Y Hospital where I hear they have a newer machine?' or 'I feel a bit embarrassed to ask, Doctor, but my wife was wondering if her results could have been confused with somebody else's?' or 'And another thing, the technician who carried out the tests, do you think he could have made a mistake? He did not look very experienced to me,' or 'What if we paid to have the tests repeated privately?'

I arranged to see them again and told them that the EEG machine was in good order, the results were not mislaid, the technician was competent and, yes, they could have the tests repeated privately but in my view this would be a waste of money. To which Mrs J replied, 'Can you please say that all again, just *once* more?'

I recalled my previous experiences of patients suffering from *folie de doute* and, remembering that the more you reassure them the worse they become, I decided on a new and dramatically different approach. Doctors are trained on the whole to be kind and reassuring people, which is appropriate in most cases but Mrs J was different. She had trawled up and down Harley Street looking for second opinions. She had forced her long-suffering husband to telephone for reassurance for her at least five times every week. She was going to have to learn to live with her *doubt*: to see that she could cope without the kindness and the reassuring magic of doctors who listened to her. I explained instead the dangers of further reassurance in her case and got her to agree that if she were to ask again I would reply: 'That kind of question is not getting you anywhere. We have agreed that I would not answer if you demand reassurance.'

She looked sad and resigned at this point but said she would try to keep to this treatment plan: 'You mean every time I think of having Alzheimer's I am not supposed to ask anyone for reassurance?'

Her husband, a retired bank manager, looked very worried: 'You mean I am not allowed to reassure her either! What am I supposed to do when she asks me about her fear of losing her memory?'

'You say the same as me.'

One week later he telephoned: 'It's no good, Doctor. She forced me to take her to Harley Street to see another doctor and have the tests repeated. But now we can't afford to keep going privately. Will you see us again?'

I agreed to see them but on condition that I did not provide reassurance about her fear. After that she gradually improved but I always had the suspicion that it was a battle for her not to give in to her addiction for reassurance from doctors. However, when her *folie de doute* came under more control, it was possible to work on this sad woman's problems. She began to talk of her loss of role as a mother since her children grew up. Her sadness became worse after her husband retired. Fear of losing her memory had taken over her life and she had developed the role of patient which necessitated continual medical reassurance.

Similar principles of being cruel to be kind were used in 1903 by a French psychologist, Pierre Janet, to treat a patient with obsessional rituals and are described in the following quotation:

> The person who assists in the performance of these actions has a very complicated part to play. He must aid in the performance of the action without actually doing it himself, although the latter would be very much easier; and he must do his utmost to conceal his own contribution to the action, for it is essential that the patient should feel he does the action himself and does it unaided. *The guide has chosen the action, has overcome the patient's hesitations, and has taken the responsibility . . . by continual repetition to perform the action; by words of encouragement at every sign of success however insignificant, for encouragement will make the patient realize these little successes, and will stimulate him with the hope aroused by glimpses of greater successes in the future.*[4]

In the case of Mrs J her reassurance-seeking can be seen as a kind of ritual which she felt compelled to repeat. 'The patient's hesitations' in her case were her *doubts* about her memory for which she was continually seeking reassurances. Similarly her 'hope [was] aroused by glimpses of greater success in future'.

When I had not heard from her for a week, she telephoned to say: 'My GP telephoned me to see if I was all right. I guess he must have been so surprised not to hear from me!' But after a month she telephoned me again: 'Could you just tell me once more that those tests were OK?'

'I can tell you one thing for certain, Mrs J. If I reassure you now in the way you want and break our agreed therapy plan, you will never get over this doubting madness we have spoken of.'

It has been a year since I have heard from Mrs J and in my

own sceptical way I thought that she had probably found someone else to prescribe the magic of medical listening to which she had become so addicted. My scepticism proved groundless when I met her general practitioner at a medical meeting. He was able to tell me that she had not succumbed and, over time, had visited him and other doctors less. Despite fears about her memory, she *had* apparently remembered what I had taught her.

AIDS phobia: the disease phobia of our century

Tom seemed to have everything going for him. He was twenty-nine years old and engaged to be married. He had been head boy at school, successful at university, and now he had a good job in marketing. The problem started when he was listening to the radio and his regular programme was followed by a government health promotion bulletin which aimed to make young people more aware of the problem of AIDS. He was only half listening but thought the bulletin said that if you had a rash or any unusual lumps or bumps on your body this could be an early sign of AIDS. He then became convinced that he did have some lumps in his groin and made an early appointment to see his doctor. 'Nothing to worry about. Just normal lymph nodes', was the verdict.

Tom was relieved at first, but then he started to worry again. He dared not discuss his real anxiety with his fiancée. How could he be *certain* that his doctor was right? He remembered that the radio bulletin had emphasized that the high-risk groups included homosexuals and intravenous drug-users, but neither of these applied in his case. Nor was he sexually promiscuous. But then he began to think of the one time he had had unprotected sexual intercourse two years before he met his fiancée. The girl was still a casual acquaintance and the source of slight embarrassment to Tom when they met. The thought then plagued him: could this girl have given him AIDS?

Tom was inspecting his body daily for lumps and rashes, and as he was an eczema sufferer he tended to have a rather blotchy skin. As his anxiety levels rose, he could not resist a visit to his doctor. 'Just your eczema, old chap. Don't worry, just use the lotion I have prescribed.'

This time the reassurance lasted only till Tom was outside the doctor's surgery. He then telephoned his ex-girlfriend and arranged a meeting. Tom wanted to have a close look at her: had she lost weight? Could he see any rashes or lumps? She *seemed* perfectly well and this gave him some relief from anxiety. Weeks went by but then the anxiety built up again. How could he be *sure* that the girl was not incubating AIDS and that he had caught the disease after his indiscretion? The fact that he kept getting these ideas, despite realizing their irrationality, shows how close this illness phobia is to obsessive-compulsive disorder where repetitive ideas intrude. Tom showed many truly phobic features: he had never listened to the radio bulletin about AIDS again and avoided reading about AIDS in newspapers and magazines. He could not bring himself to go to a clinic for sexually transmitted disease, nor would he have an AIDS test. He was becoming increasingly depressed.

Tom tried to get me to reassure him that he did not have AIDS. He looked like a man in torment, the torment of someone lost in the struggle to rescue himself but failing to do so. It was clear that he was tense and ill at ease, and it was very tempting to reassure him. I could see that this reassurance would be short-lived and that the problem was his fear that he *might* have AIDS which had to be handled differently from the easy way of responding to his request for reassurance. He had already concluded that his chances of having the disease were slight, but he could not live with the uncertainty.

I explained how avoidance leads to an increase in phobic fear and together we devised an anti-avoidance strategy.

'If facing up to it is so important, I guess I had better listen to the whole of that radio bulletin right through. The trouble is I might be out at the time it's broadcast.'

'Come on, Tom ... That looks to me like an excuse for further avoidance. How about tape-recording the programme?'

The next time he came in a state of great anxiety: 'I have taped the programme but I'm too scared to listen to it!' He dumped a cassette tape on my desk as some kind of trophy. He agreed to play it then and there, using my machine. It was clearly easier for Tom to face the phobia first with me in the room. Afterwards he had less difficulty playing it alone at home. His next homework task was to get some reading material on AIDS and he picked up a leaflet from his local chemists. Once again, he put it on the desk for my approval. And then he managed to read it with my encouragement before taking it home to read again. He also agreed not to go to his doctor for reassurance about rashes or lumps, although he could go for any other medical treatment.

The last time I heard from Tom was after his marriage. He wrote to say that he was no longer worried about anything and was not depressed. Did I want to see him again to 'check that all was well'? I replied that I would be happy to see him again, but that I could live with the uncertainty of not seeing him again if he could.

Flying phobia

Adrian was a 27-year-old unmarried civil engineer. He worked for a large, successful firm in London. Recently he had been promoted and asked to take responsibility for a job which required frequent visits to Amsterdam for meetings with the firm's clients. Adrian had a four-year history of fearing plane travel and had so far managed to keep this secret by arranging meetings for Monday mornings, travelling to Amsterdam by boat and train on the Sunday. He worried that if his problem became known his career would be jeopardized as his bosses would think him 'a nervous wreck'.

Adrian's problem had begun when he was returning to England from a holiday in India. The flight had been particularly turbulent and he remembered details of a similar aircraft being involved in a crash a few months previously, which made him feel anxious and nauseous. Since then, he had felt unable to travel by plane unless he took diazepam (prescribed by his GP) and alcohol to induce almost total amnesia for the journey. He realized that he could not do this if he was travelling to attend a business meeting.

Adrian agreed to start a programme of treatment which involved visiting the airport every evening to watch passengers checking in their luggage and aircraft land and take off. He was asked to imagine that he was actually about to travel and to wait there until his anxiety subsided. It was explained that taking alcohol or tranquillizers were forms of avoidance and, although initially reducing anxiety, in the longer term they strengthened and increased his fear.

Ten days after this initial assessment, the therapist received a phone call from Adrian at the airport. He reported that initially he had felt extremely anxious and nauseous but that this had improved on subsequent visits. One of the airlines was offering day-trips to an unknown destination and Adrian asked the therapist to accompany him on a flight.

On the day of the arranged flight the therapist met Adrian at the airport. He appeared anxious and rated his anxiety as 6 on an 8-point scale. He said that previously he would have gone immediately to the bar 'to settle his nerves' when he felt anxious, but he managed to stay in the queue to check in to the flight and then went through to the departure lounge. The destination was Cologne, just over an hour's flying time which, with the delays and return journey, would allow a sufficient period for Adrian's anxiety to reduce.

When the flight was called Adrian developed symptoms of panic. He appeared flushed, sweaty and tremulous, and said that he felt he had made a mistake. He wanted to leave the airport, return home and then continue practising his visits to the airport before attempting a flight.

The therapist pointed out: 'I can see that you are extremely anxious and realize how unpleasant it must be. However, if you go home now, it will be much more difficult for you the next time. Although you feel very anxious now, you'll remember the first time you came to the airport when you were also quite panicky. No matter how dreadful you feel now, the feeling will pass as long as you carry on.'

Adrian stood still and did not appear to be about to run from the lounge. He was breathing very rapidly and this hyperventilation was contributing to his discomfort. Instructions for taking slow deep breaths were given to him: 'I see that you are breathing very rapidly and shallowly. What I would like you to do is to put your hand on your stomach. You should be able to feel it moving in and out if you are breathing correctly, using your diaphragm. Now, drop your shoulders and try to relax and keep them still. You don't need to use your shoulders if you are breathing correctly.'

Adrian slowed his breathing and said that he was feeling a little better. There was an announcement for remaining passengers to board the aircraft and Adrian agreed to do so. The flight was moderately turbulent and Adrian reported that he wanted a drink when the air hostess came round with the bar but realized that it would make his problem worse. He was less anxious by the time he reached Cologne. On the return flight Adrian was much more confident. He asked if he could change seats to look at the clouds and the view. When we were landing, he said that he was actually enjoying the flight.

After this session Adrian arranged to fly alone to Amsterdam for a business meeting. At our six-month post-treatment follow-up, he was flying regularly to Europe and had recently booked a holiday to California. He reported that he still avoided alcohol before or during a flight as he felt that any feeling of light-headedness increased his anxiety. Adrian's success illustrates how even one session of therapist-aided exposure can effect a significant and lasting change in phobic anxiety. Not all phobias are dealt with as easily and quickly however.

Blood phobia

Clarissa, a 35-year-old married woman, was referred to the clinic with an extreme fear of any medical or dental treatment. For years she had avoided the medical profession, but recently she had forced herself to see her general practitioner as she had a marked and sudden abdominal swelling. She was referred to her local hospital and had taken 40mg of diazepam to lessen her anxiety before going there. Her gynaecologist advised a laparotomy operation to remove a large ovarian cyst but Clarissa had refused to re-attend the hospital or to visit her general practitioner. Indeed, she was reluctant to come to a psychiatric clinic and needed reassurance that it was quite separate from the general hospital and that no medical equipment would be evident.

Her fear had begun at the age of fourteen when she gave a blood sample following a routine medical examination at school. She felt anxious, nauseous and light-headed. The medical officer had gruffly told her to pull herself together and the nurse had then held her arm tightly to prevent her from moving. The blood sample was taken and she had fainted immediately afterwards. From then on she felt faint whenever she visited her general practitioner or a hospital. This had deteriorated over the years until she avoided going altogether. She had painful dental decay as she had not visited the dentist for ten years.

The assessment interview was complicated by Clarissa's extreme fear. Through much of it, she clutched a sick bowl, lying flat on the examination couch. She frequently retched and complained of feeling faint. Luckily her husband, Frank, was able to supply many of the details.

I explained to Clarissa how phobias of blood, injury and medical interventions were often different from other phobias because the anxiety reaction causes a slowing, rather than an increase, in heart rate. This could cause fainting, so the therapy would start with Clarissa lying down. As she progressed with exposure, and her physiological responses lessened, she would be raised gradually into an upright position. Because she was extremely anxious, I emphasized that nothing would be done without her prior consent or to trick her in any way. Frank agreed to act as co-therapist.

Clarissa's main target was to have her laparotomy operation. We made a list of some goals, starting with having her blood pressure taken. By working systematically through the list, Clarissa was able eventually to cope with her admission to hospital for the operation which probably saved her life.

Death phobia

Douglas, a 22-year-old man, had suffered from panic attacks since childhood. In an attack he felt 'unreal, as if I'm not really here. I think I am going to swallow my tongue, although I realize this is a silly idea, and then that I will lose control of myself.'

The panic attacks had worsened for no apparent reason about three months previously. The symptoms prevented Douglas fully enjoying life as he dreaded the attacks although they did not unduly interfere with his job as a bricklayer. He lived at home with his parents and had a reasonable social life. He had recognized that alcohol brought short-term symptom relief and he was developing a reliance on beer that threatened to become a serious problem. Douglas had to learn how to face up to his symptoms rather than use alcohol to blur them. The symptom of depersonalization, in which he felt unreal, was the most distressing to him as he believed it was a symptom of serious physical illness which might cause his death.

THERAPIST: So you realize you are not the only one with this symptom. Can we now look at the evidence for this idea of yours that you are not really here, not flesh and blood?

DOUGLAS: I feel odd, sort of freaked out, as if my arms and legs don't belong to me.

THERAPIST: So the idea that your arms and legs do not belong to you leads to anxiety?

DOUGLAS: Yes.

THERAPIST: And what happens eventually?

DOUGLAS: The attack passes and normal feelings come back to my arms and legs.

THERAPIST: What does that experience suggest to you?

DOUGLAS: That the attack will pass and that it is not dangerous.

THERAPIST: So the attack is short-lived and not lethal. What do you feel causes it?

DOUGLAS: Well, I think it is just a horrible form of anxiety attack.

THERAPIST: So would you say that rather than believing that these experiences are evidence of a serious illness, another explanation could be that, in an anxiety attack, losing sensation in your limbs leads to further anxiety but without good reason as eventually the attack passes?

DOUGLAS: I suppose you are right!

THERAPIST: How could you test this theory out?

DOUGLAS: Well, I also get really anxious if I go to a party. I usually drink beforehand or I won't go at all. If I don't drink before the party this Saturday I could try to see whether I have any experiences similar to those during an attack.

Douglas was able to do this and convinced himself that his feelings of depersonalization were symptoms of anxiety, unpleasant but temporary, and with no long-term damage.

At the next session I started to help Douglas look at his fear that he might swallow his tongue during an attack. I asked what evidence he had for this belief.

DOUGLAS: Well, I feel as if I'm going to.

THERAPIST: Any other evidence?

DOUGLAS: No.

THERAPIST: Shall we look at the evidence against this belief, then?

DOUGLAS: I've never heard of anyone swallowing their tongue and although I've had this anxiety hundreds of times, I haven't swallowed it so far.

THERAPIST: That's fine but what *could* be causing it then?

DOUGLAS: Could it be a symptom of anxiety? My mouth does feel dry.

THERAPIST: That is likely as in anxiety the autonomic nervous system is overactive and the parasympathetic part of it controls the secretion of saliva by reducing its flow. This would make your mouth feel dry and may well make you feel as if you are swallowing your tongue.

DOUGLAS: That's all right as far as it goes, but I still don't see how focusing attention on my throat brings on the symptom.

THERAPIST: How could we test that out?

DOUGLAS: I could try to think very hard now about my tongue and see what happens.

THERAPIST: Let's try that as we are sitting here now. Just think about your tongue for a few minutes . . .

DOUGLAS: I see what you mean. I am now aware of sensations I didn't have a few minutes ago.
THERAPIST: Exactly! So now perhaps you can see how attention to your throat has brought about the symptom.

Douglas wrote down the rational response to each symptom and ended up with a set of cards which he found useful to carry about. These rational responses had been worked out by him as he filled in his thought diaries. Here he wrote down the negative automatic thought he experienced, the evidence for and against each thought, and the rational response to the thought. In the early stages of therapy it is often also useful to include a space for recording the external circumstances at the time the thought occurred, as well as the resultant emotion from the thought, so that the patient can recognize how thoughts affect emotions. Towards the end of therapy I often record the underlying assumption, as well as the negative automatic thoughts, so that these can be challenged.

Fear of gaining weight

I had been seeing Pauline in my outpatient clinic for some time. The problem *seemed* to be one of depression in a 36-year-old married woman who worked part-time as a dental receptionist and had two sons aged sixteen and eighteen. She was happily married and there seemed to be no easy explanation for her depression. She enjoyed her job and was so well thought of that she had been offered a full-time post. Often it takes time for a patient to reveal what they feel embarrassed or ashamed about. This disclosure came in the course of the fourth session:

PAULINE: I am not sure how I can tell you this. I find it so embarrassing.
THERAPIST: Please try.
PAULINE: I feel like one of those teenage girls you read about in women's magazines ... It is the kind of thing you expect them to do. This should not happen to a married woman like me with two grown children.
(I waited in silence for a few moments.)

PAULINE: I make myself sick. There, I have said it now. Don't you think I am disgusting? Now tell me how stupid I am!

(Pauline explained how, after gorging herself, she would go into the bathroom, put her fingers down her throat and force herself to vomit.)

THERAPIST: No, I am not disgusted. I am pleased that you were able to tell me about something that makes you disgusted with yourself and which you find embarrassing. Tell me, do you have any ideas yourself about what makes you do it?

PAULINE: I am terrified of being fat. When I look at myself in the mirror, I think my tummy sticks out. I can't stand the sight of it, so I go and eat a whole tub of ice-cream from the freezer and then make myself sick. Then I eat too much the next day and so the cycle goes on.

I asked Pauline to stand on the scales in my consulting-room and a strange thing happened. She jumped off the scales as soon as they had registered her weight and dashed into a corner of the room. This is just the kind of reaction one sees when a spider phobic patient is confronted with a spider. The scales had registered 44 kilograms – well below the weight for someone her height, yet Pauline was convinced she weighed too much. When I examined her, it was clear that she was emaciated and I was shocked to see that she had concealed her true weight beneath multiple layers of clothing.

After some discussion she agreed to keep a dietary diary, a detailed day-by-day account of everything she ate. It would serve the dual function of making Pauline aware of exactly what she ate, as well as keeping a record for me to review with her. When we did so, it was soon clear that she had a habit of eating vast amounts of ice-cream whenever she felt upset and this led directly to the vomiting.

THERAPIST: Your dietary diary shows a clear pattern. What do you think we can do about the ice-cream?

PAULINE: You can't expect me to give that up!

THERAPIST: Come on, Pauline. That is *exactly* what I expect you to do of course. But I know it is easier said than done.

Can I suggest that you label the container in your freezer with something like THIS ICE-CREAM IS NOT FOR YOU, PAULINE. KEEP YOUR HANDS OFF!

PAULINE: OK, I'll give it a try but I don't think it is going to work.

Two weeks later she appeared in my consulting-room, saying: 'I can't do it. Even if I stop the ice-cream, I have to eat something else to excess. That makes my tummy stick out and then I have to vomit again. I can't bear the sight of my body!' Pauline's striking blue eyes filled with tears as she explained her predicament: the more she ate, the more anxious she became. She eventually agreed to a course of treatment in hospital, regular meals three times each day and she was not allowed to leave her bed until she had eaten them. Kind nurses explained the importance of staying in bed so that she did not burn up calories and encouraged her to eat. In this way Pauline gradually learned to tolerate putting on weight. She joined group-therapy sessions with other patients who had eating disorders and realized that, although she was older than average, she had much in common with patients suffering from bulimia nervosa. As her weight increased, she was allowed more freedom to exercise: firstly only short walks in the grounds of the hospital and, later on, further afield to a local park. By the end of a six-week period she had reached 52.7 kilograms. With her weight gain came an expected improvement in her feelings of depression.

We could then try to find out what made Pauline so upset that she felt she had to eat. Her dietary diary indicated that her eating was worse on the days she was *not* working.

PAULINE: Yes, I guess you are right, Doctor. When bored, it looks as if I'm more likely to overeat. And I never have a chance to vomit at work as I'm just too busy!

THERAPIST: What if you took the full-time job you have been thinking about?

PAULINE: Yes, I think I would like that. As my children have grown up, I have felt less and less needed at home. I now feel at a loose end on the days I am on my own.

Pauline did follow this up and was very well the last time I saw her. She weighed herself on the scales with none of the fear she had initially shown.

Eating disorders are a common problem in the western world and, generally, they have not been amenable to medical or traditional psychotherapeutic approaches. Behavioural treatment packages, developed in the 1960s, were more successful and consisted of four key elements:

1 Description of the behaviour to be controlled. For Pauline, the key to this was her daily diary listing the amount of food and the time and circumstances of eating it.
2 Modification and control of the discriminatory stimuli that control eating. Patients are asked to confine their eating to one room, to use distinctive table-settings and to make eating a 'pure' experience unaccompanied by other activities. In hospital Pauline could not watch television, nor was she allowed to read, when she was eating.
3 Development of techniques to control the act of eating. For example, marking the box containing her ice-cream. Other techniques include: counting each mouthful of food, putting down cutlery after each mouthful, leaving some food on the plate at the end of a meal.
4 Prompt reinforcement of behaviours which delay or control eating. Reinforcement is a term used in psychology, applied to an event which makes it more likely that one event will follow another. When Pauline had managed *not* to vomit for a day, she was encouraged to reward herself with a small present – such as a magazine or flowers. We discussed how some women's magazines with their articles on dieting and photographs of fashionably thin models give the message that thinness is associated with glamour and sexual attractiveness.

In general these behavioural approaches were used to good effect in Pauline's treatment and illustrate how, in some cases, eating disorders can be similar to phobias.

Bridge phobia

Of all strange things that I learned in medical school, my experience of being on Hungerford Bridge must be one of the most unusual.

The cadaver on the glass-topped table had been of a woman who died in her fifties. To dissect each part of her body systematically, we had begun, my colleague and I, to strip away all the fatty tisues from her back to reveal the trapezoid muscle. I thought of how she might have used the muscle to straighten her back after lifting a grandchild. Had she had children? How had she come to give her body to this medical school? Then the smell of the formalin became so overpowering that I left the dissecting-room odours to walk over Hungerford Bridge, a few minutes away from my medical school.

From the middle of the bridge I could see the Festival Hall and tall office blocks, with the oily waters of the Thames below. Behind, I could feel the vibrations of the trains to and from Charing Cross station. They passed so close that it was almost like being on the train, yet I was standing on the bridge, suspended above water. I soon forgot the dissecting-room and its smells were replaced by those of the river and the railway. Not a relaxing place, but a distracting one.

This distracting quality was just what I later recommended as a treatment for Bob who consulted me for help with a severe and disabling phobia. He was a very pleasant, cheerful young man who had become concerned that he would lose his job because of his fear of train travel. It had started one day when the train he had been travelling on stopped on a bridge.

'I had this sudden feeling of dizziness. I thought I was going to be sick. My legs went like jelly. My heart was pounding. I couldn't bear to look out of the train window, as this made everything worse. I closed my eyes and prayed for what seemed an eternity for the train to move off the bridge. I didn't dare open my eyes, yet, at the same time, I felt drawn to do so. Eventually the train started and I calmed down.

'The problem then was that I feared going on the train again, in case it would stop on the bridge. I knew this was likely in the rush hour on my usual route, so I began varying my route and travelling at different times, although this was very inconvenient. I started to be late for work for the first time in my life.

'The trouble was that I still had the residual fear that the train *might* stop on the bridge, as this possibility could never be completely ruled out. It was then that I started staying off work for days at a time. This is why I have come to see you.'

Bob's case was a clear example of classically learned avoidance of a specific feared situation. He knew it did not make sense to avoid train travel, but getting him back to it would not be easy. I needed a way to help him face the situation long enough for habituation to occur, and then for him to repeat this as often as necessary. I remembered my own experience of avoidance of the stench of the dissecting room on Hungerford Bridge and described the approach to Bob. He said, 'It sounds a good idea, but there is no way I could walk to the middle of that bridge on my own. It is long and narrow, with the river on one side and the trains rushing by on the other. No way. If someone came with me, though, I just might do it – if you really think it would help.'

The following Sunday Bob, his parents and his girlfriend went to the South Bank, close to Hungerford Bridge. They encouraged Bob to walk across the bridge with them. He reported back at the next session.

BOB: It wasn't quite as bad as I thought it would be, but this was because they were with me.

THERAPIST: Very good, so far! How about making a plan to separate from the others when you have walked a little way across the bridge?

BOB: You mean go on my own with all those trains passing right by. Not on your life!

THERAPIST: You did it with the others there. Why do you think that made it so much easier?

BOB: I am not sure . . . Maybe having someone to turn to *if* the worst should happen?

THERAPIST: If you had your relatives in sight, without them actually being alongside, perhaps you would still have that safe feeling?

The next weekend Bob went again to the South Bank with his parents and girlfriend. Encouraged to venture a few yards on to the bridge alone, he was amazed at how easy this was. He then went a few more yards and gradually he was able to get to the middle of the bridge on his own.

BOB: It was a cold blustery day and I felt sorry for them out there, waving to give me encouragement. I suggested they went for coffee in the Festival Hall as I knew I could beat it alone at that stage. I walked to the middle of the bridge, as you said, and just waited there by myself for half an hour. By then I knew I had cracked it!

Bob was able to travel to work every day by train after this as trains and bridges no longer held any fear for him.

Phobias of bridges are similar in many ways to agoraphobia as Isaac Marks has pointed out:

When standing in the street or on a train platform, agoraphobics may feel drawn to jump beneath an approaching bus or train and so have to look away from the oncoming vehicle. This fear is related to the impulse normal people often feel to jump when looking down from a great height. Fear of heights is found in some agoraphobics and is countered by withdrawal from the edge of such heights or by avoiding them completely. Bridges evoke similar fear, especially long, narrow bridges with open sides high above a river. If there is a waist-high parapet between the subject and the edge of the cliff or bridge, the fear is diminished.[5]

Fear of being enclosed

'Me go in an attic? I would never do that. I'm a famous claustrophobic.'

– Woody Allen, August 1992

Although this phobia is the other side of the coin to agoraphobia, there are similarities to those cases of agoraphobia described in chapter 2. John had been through a frightening experience ten years earlier when a lift full of people became stuck between floors. It was about an hour before they were released and since then John avoided lifts and would not travel by train in case it stuck in a tunnel. He had anxiety symptoms in confined spaces, including small rooms if the door was shut. More recently this fear extended to aeroplanes, and John was worried that it would prevent him from going abroad which his job as an architect sometimes demanded. 'I ought to have forgotten that incident in the lift ten years ago. Common sense tells me that it is unlikely that I will become trapped again in a similar way.'

Unfortunately phobias do not have much to do with common sense as part of their definition is that they *are* irrational. Treatment in John's case involved, of course, teaching him to enter small and confined spaces until his anxiety subsided. As with the other cases, how this was done involved *negotiating* with him.

THERAPIST: I don't expect you would be able to go in a lift today, but can you think of any confined area that we could use to give you something like the experience of being in a lift?

JOHN: There is a cupboard under the stairs at home ... I don't think I could go into it ...

THERAPIST: How about if you left the door open, and your wife or a friend stayed within earshot? Although anxiety *is* unpleasant, it won't harm you and the longer you stay in the cupboard the more your fear will eventually go away.

The next session began with John reporting his success at remaining in the cupboard, finally with no one else in the house *and* with the door shut. So far, so good. The problem of tackling the big one – lifts – proved more difficult.

John explained, 'The thing here is that I have no control over the lift: it could plummet to earth once I have got in, or I might get stuck again as I did before. I don't think I am ever going to be able to go in a lift again.' When John said this, I thought we ought to do some work on these thoughts. He *knew* it was unlikely that he would have a repetition of his earlier bad experience in a lift but he needed something to remind him that this was so and to guide his thoughts into more helpful and productive channels. Talking alone with the therapist is not enough and I ask my patients to write some cue cards to take to read to themselves. John's cards looked like this:

1A This lift could plummet to earth once I get in.

1B Statistically this is most unlikely. When it did get stuck that time before, nothing terrible happened to me and I just had to wait to be rescued.

2A When I get in a lift I feel hot and uncomfortable and this leads to the most unpleasant sensation that I am going to faint.

2B Feeling hot and uncomfortable in a confined space is quite normal. Feeling faint when I am hot and anxious is also normal. It happens to soldiers on parade on a hot day. Sometimes they pass out but they come round after lying down for a while. When I am hot and anxious my heart rate increases and my heart pump is not so efficient. This means less blood gets to my head and so I feel faint.

3A Will I ever get in a lift again?

3B The way to prove that I can is to *do* it and remember the golden rule: practice makes perfect.

Time and again I have been told by patients that they will not be able to confront whatever they are phobic about. But I have had the moving, almost miraculous, experience of finding that if I go with them they *can* indeed face the situation. John and I went to a lift in the hospital building.

'You want me to get in with you when the lift arrives at this floor?' John asked.

'Yes, please try to get in with me.'

It was as simple as that. John got in the lift and read his cue cards. He was soon able to go in lifts alone and later on to travel by aeroplane. He always took his cue cards and, as far as I know, has them in his pocket to this day.

It could be argued that complex psychological factors were at work here. Did I represent someone in whom he could have complete confidence? Why otherwise had he not run a mile when the lift arrived or at least refused to enter? Why had he not showed great anxiety when he was in the lift, as, for example, Laura had done while facing her plastic snake? There are mysteries about phobias as varied as human nature itself.

Fear of farting

In my day-to-day clinical work it is not unusual for the problem a patient initially comes along with *not* to be the problem that he or she is really concerned about. Clara, a 36-year-old house-wife, was said to be agoraphobic. Indeed, she did have many of the classic symptoms: she dreaded going out, avoided public transport, disliked crowded places and social settings. But there was something about Clara that I could not immediately put a finger on that worried me. Behaviour therapy is not just a straightforward, even simple-minded, approach where you 'flood' the patient with whatever they fear or avoid most, while preventing them from escaping the feared situation. Most therapists who work with agoraphobic patients know how complicated it can be and successful treatment demands an understanding of people.

Clara would giggle in an embarrassed way. Phobic patients are often shy and find it humiliating to talk about their problem but Clara seemed almost mortified. She had the greatest diffi-culty telling me that she was afraid to go into social settings in case she passed wind. This was a problem she had since child-hood: 'I remember passing wind in the school assembly when I was ten years old. I was so embarrassed and afraid that others would notice that I stayed away from school for several months after that.'

I discovered that Clara had coped reasonably well until she had had to take her own child to school. The fear recurred and led her to avoid visiting her child's school. More and more situations began to be avoided until the full-blown agoraphobic syndrome developed. Freud in 1889 had described a similar case where a forgotten childhood experience was relevant to a phobia in adulthood (the case of Frau Emmy von N.), and hypnosis, the treatment then in vogue, was used. Nowadays we have abandoned hypnosis because it is an unreliable therapy which does not produce lasting effects in phobic disorders.

Clara's treatment was first directed at the beliefs surrounding her anxiety about passing wind.

THERAPIST: Tell me, Clara, what is it that is so bad for you about passing wind?

CLARA: I'm terrified that people will look round and think how awful of me to have done that!

THERAPIST: In the first place, how can you be sure they will know it's you, and also can you be sure they will consider it so awful?

I explained to her the physiological fact that *everybody* farts half a litre a day, and that the gas is produced by fermentation of our dietary carbohydrate by normal intestinal bacteria. To get her to see the humorous side, I told her about le Petomaine, a man in the 1890s who was a star turn at the Moulin Rouge. He could snuff out a candle by farting and with a repertoire of tricks made his living by exaggerating the very activity that Clara was so embarrassed about.

THERAPIST: So we have a situation where you could be magnifying this, building it up in your mind out of all proportion to its effect on others. You avoid risking yourself in a public situation and that leads to more avoidance.

CLARA: You mean if I faced the worst and risked feeling humiliated that could help?

Clara and I together developed a self-help exposure programme which involved her going into crowded shops, then travelling by train, and finally visiting her daughter's school and sitting in the middle of a row during a school play. After four sessions she was going alone into shops and travelling by train, things she had been unable to do for five years. After five sessions Clara went for the jackpot and braved the school play. Since then she has not looked back and, in her own words, 'this thing used to ruin my life, but never again'.

The psychoanalytic model or the purely behavioural model

would not have worked for Clara. The cognitive approach, however, helped her understand why she had avoided certain situations for all these years. It had been too embarrassing for her to describe her problem before this therapy.

6 Sexual Phobias

'Don't knock masturbation, you are talking about
sex with someone I love'

– Woody Allen, 1990

'There are frightful consequences of the heinous
sin of self-pollution'

– A popular treatise on the dangers of
masturbation, 1730

In Victorian England there was a common fear that masturbation led to masturbatory insanity. Sir John Hunter, surgeon
to St George's Hospital, London, and also to King George
III, had been ahead of his time in pointing out that masturbation itself was not harmful but that the guilty feelings associated with it could be. Now, in our own day, the great pres-
sures on sexual performance can lead to different kinds of
anxiety for men and women. I see many patients where fear
of normal sexual activity is so strong that it amounts to a
sexual phobia.

In this century the culture of repression has given way to a
consumer cult of choice. Such books as *The Joy of Sex* by Alex
Comfort[1] and sex-therapy videos such as *The Lover's Guide* by
Andrew Stanway have meant that *information* about techniques
is widely available. But information alone is not enough to help
the sexually phobic. Steven Soderbergh's film *Sex, Lies and
Videotape* tells how an impotent young man attempts to deal
with his phobia of sexual intercourse by making videotapes of
young women describing their sexual experiences and fantasies.
Until a new partner allows him to talk about *his* problems to
her, he fails. This powerful film examines some of the complex-
ities of human sexual activity which we cannot begin to tackle

here. However, readers with particular sexual phobias or fears may find the following case material helpful.

Problems specific to women

Fear of sexual intercourse: the case of the virgin wife

Spasm of the vagina, technically called vaginismus, can lead to painful intercourse or, in some cases, the impossibility of sexual intercourse, which resulted in one of my patients remaining a virgin many years after her marriage.

Mary was a healthy-looking woman of thirty-eight who enjoyed working as a nursing manager. She had a B.Sc. degree in biology and obviously knew all she needed to know to become pregnant. She had a full social life and was a leading light in her local dramatic club. She looked as if she had never had a day's physical illness and, before seeing me, had no need to consult anyone for a psychological reason. What prompted her to visit me was that she and her husband wanted a family. They had been married for ten years and had been having tests for 'infertility' for the last year, unable to explain that full sexual intercourse never occurred. The most recent investigation suggested by the gynaecologist posed a serious problem for them. The post-coital examination involves the wife visiting her gynaecologist the morning after sexual intercourse so that a vaginal swab can be taken. The semen is examined to see if there is any incompatibility between it and the vaginal fluid that might cause infertility.

MARY: You will think me completely stupid or completely hysterical.
THERAPIST: Well, let us try and work this out together. Stupid? I hardly think someone with a good science degree can be that. One way of looking at neurotic problems is to think of them as very intelligent people behaving stupidly. What do you think?
MARY: If I am not stupid, then I must be a total neurotic wreck, a total hysteric. I am probably incurable and you can do nothing for me.

THERAPIST: Hang on a minute. Hysteria, as I am sure you know, implies that unconscious factors are at work and this may be the case here. Before jumping to that conclusion though, I would like to hear a few more details. You told me earlier that you and your husband had a good, basically loving relationship?

MARY: Yes, Doctor, we do get on well in general and are very close.

THERAPIST: I am sorry to have to ask such intimate questions, but if I am to be able to help you I need to know exactly where the difficulty arises. This means asking you to explain what happens when you and your husband make love.

MARY: Well, we have fallen into a pattern over the years. And, in fact, we both enjoy it this way. I stimulate my husband's penis with my hands, using a lubricant. He stimulates my genital area. We both give and receive pleasure this way at the same time. Whenever he has tried to penetrate me in the past, I go all tense inside and we both end up frustrated and annoyed. So we just gave up trying a few years ago. I thought somehow we might be able to do it properly one time and then I would get pregnant. Now I feel the pressure is really on for me to perform so that the stupid test can be done, and I feel a proper fool.

I explained to Mary that feeling under pressure to perform sexually is the worst possible thing. We agreed that she should cancel the test and I proposed the standard psychological therapy used in cases of fear of intercourse, sensate focus, first described by the American sex therapists Masters and Johnson.[2]

Despite criticism of the scientific merit of their work, Masters and Johnson produced dramatically successful results, impossible to ignore. Practitioners were swept along on a wave of enthusiasm for this new treatment, then applied by many who knew little about it and by many who believed it was a panacea. Inevitable disappointments followed but now we know that these techniques can be modified for patients with sexual difficulties. The basic treatment consists of the following steps:

- a ban on sexual intercourse during the treatment
- education about sex, basic anatomy and physiology of sexuality; exploring the couple's sexual vocabulary and providing a vocabulary for future sessions
- teaching relaxation
- non-genital sensate focus
- genital sensate focus
- penetration (initially without pelvic thrusting), generally performed in the female superior or lateral positions for most problems except for male retarded ejaculation
- use of different sexual positions and resumption or commencement of full sexual life.

In Mary's case sensate focus was carried out along these lines. After I had diagnosed vaginismus, I asked permission to contact her gynaecologist to establish whether she did indeed have no anatomical or physiological disorder to prevent normal intercourse. One of the rare anatomical problems is where the woman's hymen is too tough to be penetrated by the penis, and in these cases a surgical procedure has to be carried out. However, Mary's gynaecologist said she was quite normal anatomically, but described to me the typical response of a patient with vaginismus: she contracted her inner thigh muscles when he approached her and made the vaginal examination very difficult to perform. He was a caring, sensitive surgeon who had seen vaginismus before, so I asked him what he proposed to do. He answered, 'She is a psychological case. You are the psychiatrist. *You* treat her!'

At the next consultation I suggested to Mary that she perform self-examination and self-exploration exercises, using a hand-mirror, after she had a warm bath, was relaxed and comfortable, with no fear of interruption. I also gave her instructions on Kegel's exercises, the contractions and relaxation of the pubo-coccygeus muscles. The easiest way to explain these was to ask her to stop mid-stream when she passed urine. Once she had done this, she could try the same movement when not passing water. If she made it slowly, she would become aware that she could contract these muscles to varying degrees. When they are fully contracted, the muscles surrounding the anus are involved and can be relaxed so that just the anterior muscles are contracting, which in their turn can be fully relaxed. The purpose of these exercises in vaginismus is to increase the woman's awareness of the muscles involved in the problem and to establish some control over them.

At the second individual session Mary reported some success with the Kegel exercises and self-examination. She was asked to start self-exploration and to try to monitor pleasurable sensations, including gently rubbing her clitoral region and to continue anything pleasurable. When she was feeling completely relaxed and enjoying the sensations of touching herself, she was asked to try to insert the tip of her little finger into her vagina using a lubricant jelly. While doing this, she should perform some Kegel exercises a few times and monitor the effect on her vagina. Once she could do this, she was asked to gradually insert more and more of her finger and, if she could before her next visit, to try with her ring finger and, later, her middle finger.

When Mary arrived for her next appointment a week later, she reported that although she had managed to insert each of her fingers in turn, she was still anxious about it. With further practise and the use of a relaxation tape, this anxiety diminished. She was next asked to practise inserting the smallest size of tampon into her vagina and to keep it there for up to two hours.

Three more sessions were needed, by which time Mary could happily insert three fingers and also a medium tampon into her vagina. Before this stage was reached, a joint session had been held with Mary and her husband and they had started non-genital sensate focus.

Now the couple was given instructions for genital sensate focus. Mary was to demonstrate to her husband how she was best aroused and how to gradually work up to the insertion of his smallest finger. At her own speed, they could move on to larger fingers and eventually to more than one finger.

After three weeks of genital sensate focus Mary reported that she had reached orgasm and that her husband could insert three fingers without causing her pain or distress. The next stage was to move on to penile penetration without movement, with Mary in the superior position. When this was achieved I asked them to try penetration plus gentle pelvic thrusts and, thereafter, alternative sexual positions. The couple continued to progress well with the therapy and Mary did become pregnant. Ten years' fear of sexual intercourse had been overcome by a twelve-week course of therapy.

Lack of orgasm in women

Much has been written on the subject of the female orgasm. My advice is confined only to women whose *fear* of sexual activity leads to problems in this area. To achieve orgasm a woman has to be relaxed about her body and to have a realistic outlook. One patient consulted me because she had read in a woman's magazine that *multiple* orgasms were the norm and she could only achieve single ones. The treatment in her case was simply pointing out she had been misled. Women with sexual phobias often are too frightened to obtain helpful information about normal sexual activity.

I would like to describe the normal sexual response and show how fears can be allayed by sensate focus. Masters and Johnson's work first undertook an extensive study of normal human sexual response under a number of conditions. For example, different age groups, whether the women had had children or not, their previous sexual experience, and their sexual situation. Among their findings one of the most revolutionary for the time was that men and women are remarkably similar in the changes which take place during sexual activity: their four-stage model of sexual response. The first stage is excitement, during which women experience an increase in the flow of blood in the blood vessels around the vagina accompanied by an increase in the normal vaginal lubrication. The second stage involves higher sexual arousal and the clitoris is enlarged. The third stage is orgasm itself which most women find difficult to describe: it involves a rhythmic contraction of muscles in the genital area with an intensely pleasurable feeling described as 'like the earth moving'. Finally, there is a slow return to normal: the resolution phase.

Sensate focus treatment

Sensate focus is a way of helping couples, fearful of sexual activity, go through the various stages of sexual arousal.

Michael and Lorraine, a 23-year-old couple, had been living together for two years when they were referred to the clinic. Lorraine had never enjoyed sex and would only tolerate Michael's sexual approaches to her once every two months or so. This was unbearable for Michael who felt rejected and unloved. There were frequent arguments as Lorraine began to refuse *any* physical contact, fearing it might lead to a sexual advance.

From the age of five, Lorraine had gone to a convent girl's school. Ultimately she gained good examination results and went to teacher's training college. She had had no sex education at home and at school a nun had explained in vague terms that women had to undergo 'humiliation' in marriage to experience the joy of having children.

Lorraine had never masturbated as she believed it was 'sinful'. At teacher's training college she met Michael and they had started dating. Their relationship had never been physically passionate although after a year she had allowed him to touch her breasts. They had not engaged in heavy petting until they had started to live together when she left college. She felt guilty about this decision, which her parents disapproved of, although she no longer felt religious. When Michael made any sexual advance to her, she felt numb with fear and hoped to end it as soon as possible. She had never experienced orgasm.

Michael, a young school teacher, was the only child of elderly parents. He had had a happy childhood and went to local state schools. Sex had been freely discussed at home but he believed that for successful sex, the man was responsible for his own and his partner's pleasure. His first sexual experience had been at the age of fifteen with a girl at school. It had not been enjoyable but later he had several casual relationships which he had found satisfying. When he was twenty, a girlfriend had commented that his penis was small and he had started to worry whether he would be able to satisfy any woman. He masturbated about twice a week to heterosexual fantasies and had done so since he was fourteen. He described his relationship with Lorraine as good and close, despite the sexual problems.

Although Michael had previously enjoyed sex, now he had become overly concerned about his sexual performance. Whenever he started to make a sexual advance, he worried about his own performance instead of relaxing and enjoying sex. And so a vicious circle was formed with Lorraine's inability to enjoy sex reinforcing Michael's own feelings of inadequacy.

We started their sex education with pictures of male and female genitalia for them to give their words for different organs and their functions, with the therapist saying these words when they were not given. They were then written down so that those words with which the couple were happy and familiar could be used throughout their therapy.

The therapist then discussed the function and physiology of the sexual organs and the mechanics of sexual intercourse. Care was taken to explain to Michael that the size of a man's penis has little to do with his ability to give sexual pleasure to his partner. In any case, a relatively small penis tends to enlarge more during erection than a larger one. Michael's faulty belief that a man was solely responsible for his own and his partner's pleasure was also discussed, as was his idea that the man should always initiate sex. Lorraine's view of sex as something which women were subjected to without any personal enjoyment was also challenged.

Relaxation instructions were given (see chapter 9) and a practice run gone through by the therapist with the couple. For homework they were asked to set aside an hour a day to lie on their bed wearing loose clothing, with soft lighting and gentle background music, to encourage a hedonistic view of sexual activity. When they were both fully relaxed they were to read from Alex Comfort's *The Joy of Sex*. Michael was reminded of the ban on intercourse and told that if he felt very sexually aroused he was to masturbate. Lorraine said that she would be happy for Michael to masturbate while lying next to her. The question of birth control was raised and Lorraine admitted that she had not liked to consult her family doctor. It was suggested that they attend a local family planning clinic to obtain information. We agreed that as they had so much homework we should not meet for three weeks.

At the third session Lorraine and Michael appeared much more at ease. Firstly, we reviewed their homework and, whereas initially she had been tense, once Lorraine realized that she could trust Michael not to try intercourse, she had found the exercises pleasant and soothing. And both said that the books were interesting and useful. Lorraine had observed Michael's pleasure during masturbation and asked if she could masturbate too, although she didn't know how. The therapist gave her a picture of female external genitalia to take home. It was suggested that she might examine her genitals, using a hand-mirror. Then, she could start to touch them and to gently rub her clitoris and insert her finger into her vagina. She should monitor her sensations and continue with whatever felt pleasant. As she did not want to masturbate in front of Michael, she could do so alone in their bedroom, lying on the bed after a warm bath and relaxation exercises.

The next stage in therapy was to introduce non-genital sensate focus. Michael and Lorraine were asked again to set aside some time every evening when they would lie together on their bed either naked or in their underwear. After their relaxation exercises, they were each to take turns in touching each other's body anywhere except Lorraine's breasts or their genitals. This gentle touching could be rubbing, stroking in circular movements or caressing, with lips and tongues, as well as fingers and palms. They were asked to try out these movements with their hands on the back of their partner's hand. Once this was done satisfactorily, the partner being fondled should say what was pleasurable or less so and what would be preferable. They were to take turns being the active participant or the recipient on a give to get basis with open communication and feedback, to practise discussing sex more freely. It was also suggested that they might like to try using lotions, baby oil or body creams to find which was best for them.

At the fourth session the couple reported that they had progressed well. Both were enjoying the non-genital sensate focus and learning more about what was exciting and pleasurable to their partner and themselves. Lorraine had been shy about giving feedback but was gradually improving. The therapist congratulated them on their progress and urged them to continue with the exercise.

Lorraine then asked if she could speak to the therapist on her own. She reported that she had enjoyed the self-exploration of her genitals but had stopped doing so when she felt that her excitement might mean 'losing control'. When asked to think of the last time this had happened and what had gone through her mind at this time, Lorraine said, 'I might lose control and go out of my mind.' This thought had immediately stopped her masturbation exercises.

It was clear that Lorraine's negative thought about losing control was severely interfering with her sexual pleasure and a cognitive approach was used to challenge these thoughts: 'Can you think of any evidence to support or refute this belief?' At the end of this exercise, Lorraine rated her belief that she might lose control and go mad at less than 5 per cent. She was willing to continue with the self-exploration programme. The therapist then asked whether she would be able to discuss her worries in front of Michael, but she felt this would be too embarrassing. Michael was brought back into the room and another appointment was made for a week ahead.

When the couple arrived for the fifth session they both looked cheerful. Lorraine immediately reported that she had masturbated on her own to orgasm. The non-genital sensate focus had also progressed well and they had both enjoyed using body lotion. Then the next stage of genital sensate focus was explained to them in an explicit way to ensure understanding and also to serve as a model of talking about sexual experience frankly.

The therapist said: 'The next stage of genital sensate focus is exactly the same as the previous exercise except that now I want you to include the genital and breast regions. Once again, you should start with relaxation exercises and take turns caressing your partner's body. You can then include the breasts and genitals. The partner being touched should tell the other what is enjoyable or what they would prefer. You can demonstrate this by guiding your partner's hands to show what gives you most pleasure.

'Michael, Lorraine will guide you as to what feels best for her. You may like to start by caressing her breasts and nipples gently, also using your lips and tongue. Then you could move to the outer and inner labia and try rubbing her clitoris before inserting your finger into her vagina if it is sufficiently lubricated. You may find it is even more enjoyable for Lorraine if you use your lips and tongue. Lorraine can guide you as to the rhythm and amount of pressure which feels best.

'Lorraine, you too should try caressing Michael's scrotum and penis. The top of the penis is particularly sensitive, so be careful that you do not press it too hard. You have watched Michael masturbate and so you know what pleases him but you may like to experiment with other movements and sensations too. Again, Michael may find this even more exciting if you also use your lips and tongue.'

Michael and Lorraine felt happy with these instructions although Lorraine was unsure about oral sex. It was explained that many couples found it extremely enjoyable and that they might like to try it even if they decided against it later. An appointment was made for the following week.

When the couple returned, they said that they had been successful in doing the exercises. Michael had experienced orgasms on each occasion but Lorraine had not done so yet. The therapist urged them to continue and explained that women were frequently slower to get aroused than men. It was particularly important that their bedroom was comfortable and that the relaxation and non-genital sensate focus exercises were followed to ensure Lorraine time for arousal.

By the seventh session both reported that they had enjoyed several sessions of genital sensate focus, both reaching orgasm, and they were keen to move on to the next stage. Penetration was then introduced to follow all the previous steps in the exercises. Lorraine was to be in the female superior position so that she felt she had greater control. Once both of them felt happy with this, Michael could try some gentle pelvic thrusts, but should stop if Lorraine felt uncomfortable and continue only when she agreed. After Lorraine and Michael had enjoyable intercourse in this way, a repertoire of sexual positions was introduced to bring variety into their sex lives. Generally, they progressed extremely well. Lorraine was concerned that she was not orgasmic during penetration although she was during genital sensate focus. It was explained that a high percentage of women cannot reach orgasm without additional direct clitoral stimulation during penetration.

This case history of Lorraine and Michael shows how even fairly deep-seated sexual problems can be treated in relatively few sessions.

Problems specific to men

As a man's sexual organs are more obvious than a woman's he can be more readily aware of a problem which he cannot conceal from his partner and so he may be more easily embarrassed and socially disadvantaged by it. The common problems that men experience are failure of erection, premature ejaculation and failure of ejaculation.

Failure of erection

It is well known that anxiety makes it difficult to get an erection. Adolescent boys have been known to prevent unwanted erections at embarrassing moments by deliberately thinking of accidents or other frightening ideas to make the erection go away.

From the four stages of arousal already described, it is clear that a man and woman have to learn to provide increasing sexual stimulation in relaxed ways. If penetrative sex induces anxiety, then manual stimulation using a lubricant can often be helpful. This can gradually lead to penetration for longer periods.

Premature ejaculation

Known as 'coming too quickly', this can be a most frustrating and embarrassing problem. Talking it over with your partner is the first step, then try to delay the time it takes to ejaculate by the stop–start technique.

Fred was referred with problems of ejaculation. He ejaculated much quicker than usual because of his anxiety. He *expected* to ejaculate prematurely, which not only led to the anticipation of failure but also to a high performance anxiety which resulted in further premature ejaculation. This problem had resulted in insufficiently long stimulation for June, his partner, to reach orgasm, further complicated by her own performance anxiety and the anticipation of not achieving orgasm before Fred ejaculated.

Over the first few weeks of treatment the therapist placed a ban on sexual intercourse and work followed on sexual education, instruction in non-genital sensate focus and the stop–start technique. When Fred was highly aroused during genital sensate focus, June was to immediately stop all stimulation and sexual activity until his arousal subsided, generally taking no longer than two minutes. They were then to start stimulation again. This exercise was to be repeated three or four times before Fred was allowed to ejaculate. He was to concentrate hard on the sensations in his penis during stimulation and signal a level of high arousal to June before reaching the point of ejaculatory inevitability. For the first week they were to use only their hands but once the exercise was fully mastered, they could try lotion to increase Fred's arousal with moist sensation more like vaginal penetration.

Failure of ejaculation

This is where a man can hold an erection for as long as he wants but cannot ejaculate inside his partner's vagina. Fear and anxiety are probably at the root of the problem, but there is an effective behavioural treatment: the woman uses vigorous manual stimulation of her partner's penis until he is close to ejaculation. He then inserts his penis to ejaculate inside her. The aim then is to move gradually in a way that does not produce anxiety to less manual and more vaginal stimulation. In this way the man ends up with most of the stimulation from vaginal intercourse.

General points about sexual phobias

Sex mostly concerns two people! This point must not be overlooked when focusing on the therapy techniques. If you are basically shy and socially phobic, then the approaches described in chapter 3 may be more appropriate for you. If there is a serious relationship difficulty between you and your partner, it would not be surprising if sex is not as good as it should be. Sex therapy is outside the scope of this book but self-help books are included in the Reading List. I have focused on couples with a heterosexual orientation but many of these techniques could be adapted and applied to homosexual couples.

A word of warning about video tapes devoted to sex therapy: not all are as well made as others. In general, it is my experience that soft porn films can make sexually phobic patients worse. One partner can be made to feel inadequate and this can lead to a vicious circle of resentment and panic. Some people are happier with illustrated books where they feel more in control of the material they are to see. But I have heard from a couple whose sex life was dramatically changed by a carefully made and sensitive sex therapy video.

You may find that in reading these cases you discover ways to help yourself. The principle in dealing with vaginal spasm is to gradually allow yourself to explore your sexual organs – one advantage of self-therapy is that you can do this in your own time. Then, the insertion of a small tampon can be tried when you feel ready. It is often suggested that sexual fantasy material can be helpful for women who cannot reach orgasm.

Difficulties with penile erection can be helped with a partner who is caring and cooperative. But premature ejaculation *can* be dealt with alone by masturbation. Here, the idea is to stimulate yourself gently and then stop just before ejaculation seems inevitable. Then start again, but stop once more when you are about to ejaculate. In this way you can teach yourself to control the time it takes to ejaculate.

Failure of ejaculation may be due to anxiety. Also, men vary enormously in what stimulation they need to reach a climax. By exploring your sexual sensations during masturbation you can discover what to pass on to your partner to make love-making more enjoyable for both of you.

In brief

- Masturbation can be used to overcome sexual anxieties and should not be considered harmful.
- Sexual phobias can be reduced with information about sexual anatomy and the four stages of sexual excitement.
- Problems specific to women include vaginal spasm and problems with orgasm.
- Problems specific to men include difficulty with erections, premature ejaculation and failure of ejaculation.
- There is often a link between specific sexual phobias and social and marital problems.
- Sexual phobias can be gradually overcome by trying techniques that are comfortable to you and your partner, and, as with other phobias, practice usually makes perfect.

7 Misconceptions

'To err is human, to forgive, divine'

– Alexander Pope

'Experience is the name one gives
to one's mistakes'

– Oscar Wilde

One of the problems with self-help is that you can go wrong. Doctors also make mistakes at times and this chapter points out some common errors to prevent you going along the wrong lines. One of the most frequent mistakes is to miss a depression because depressed people are often phobic. Phobias are often confused with something quite different – obsessive-compulsive disorder. And simple things like drinking too much coffee can cause panic attacks. Finally, there are some rare and bizarre medical conditions that mimic phobias.

Depressive illness[1]

Megan had not been out of her house for several weeks. It had started with not coping with her job as a librarian. She had suddenly lost all interest in her work, started taking time off without proper sick notes and eventually lost the job. As she was a single woman in her forties with no children, her job had been very important to her. Things then went from bad to worse and she lost all interest in food and started to sleep badly. Her neighbour found Megan in a miserable state when she brought in some shopping for her, and suggested that she visit her general practitioner for help. Megan said she was too afraid to go out and so could not get to her doctor who thought she must have agoraphobia. He asked for a visit from the local community mental health team and only then the correct diagnosis of depression was made.

The symptoms of depression to watch out for are: low mood, sleep disturbance, loss of appetite, lack of interest, a feeling of hopelessness and, in severe cases, a feeling that life is not worth living. The treatment of depression is beyond the scope of this book but self-help books are listed in the Reading List.

Obsessive-compulsive disorder[2]

'Please see this patient of mine who has not been out of the house for ten years. I am certain she has agoraphobia.' One soon learns that it is difficult to be certain of anything in medicine and I ought to have suspected something when I was told that this patient would not answer the phone. She could not get up to hospital to see me as she was agoraphobic, but why would she not answer her phone?

I eventually got her answer to this question (the home visit had been arranged through her son): 'I could not answer the phone in case you would be telephoning from . . . a certain kind of place . . . It is so hard for me to explain . . . The word begins with an H.'

I now had a strong suspicion that the diagnosis was not straightforward agoraphobia, if agoraphobia at all, and replied: 'Is it OK if *I* say this word you find so hard to say?' She nodded. I felt as if I was being made to play the kind of guessing game my young son likes: 'Is the word *hospital*?' She nodded.

THERAPIST: You don't mind if I say the word hospital, but why do *you* find it so hard?

PATIENT: Because I just *do*. It's a horrible word. It makes me feel all kind of bad and dirty and diseased. If I said the H word, I would not even be able to go out to the good supermarket in case I contaminated people.

I asked her to explain about good and bad supermarkets.

PATIENT: Well, *good* supermarkets have a good kind of feel to them because the doors have a kind of pointed bit over the top. (She drew a triangle on a piece of paper to show me what she meant.) *Bad* supermarkets do not have this shape over the top of the door. That means they are bad and I could never go in them. If I did, something terrible would happen . . . This sounds completely crazy and I know it's all so stupid. I feel embarrassed talking about it.

THERAPIST: Is there anything else you feel embarrassed about?

PATIENT: Well, I do spend a great deal of time checking any newspaper or magazine that comes through the door. I have to see if they have the H word and, if they do, I throw them away. When my son comes to visit, which is usually twice a week, I ask him to check the mail. The worst are all these advertisements for insurance schemes for private H places. You know what I mean?

I did indeed know what she meant and I was now fairly certain that this patient did not have agoraphobia but a condition known as obsessive-compulsive disorder. She had no problem at all leaving the house regularly to do her shopping at what she called her good supermarkets, and her rather weird ideas and almost mystical associations about bad supermarkets are typical of obsessive-compulsive disorder. What she did have in common with agoraphobia was her definite avoidance but it was bound up with her obsessional ideas.

There is effective behavioural and cognitive therapy for obsessive-compulsive disorder described by Judith Rapoport in *The Boy Who Could Not Stop Washing* and this treatment is often combined with the drug clomipramine.

Dirt phobia

This is not really a phobia at all but a variant of obsessive-compulsive disorder which the millionaire eccentric Howard Hughes was said to suffer from.

My patient Helen was severely disabled by not being able to touch her children, her husband or anything belonging to them. There was no clear-cut obsessional idea linked to her rituals, although she thought they might have begun after her first child was born thirteen years previously and she had tried to keep the environment sterile. She completely avoided rubbish bins and anything that had been in contact with them. She would do all her housework wearing plastic bags over her hands and her husband dealt with the rubbish bins and cleaned the lavatories. She avoided all lavatories except her own but she held herself several inches above the lavatory seat when using it. Just before her admission to hospital, she had taken to defecating in a plastic bag which she would then bury in the garden.

Helen also could not go anywhere that involved proximity to or contact with water, particularly rainwater or stagnant water, and she avoided short walks near home that crossed bridges or went anywhere near stretches of water. She could not touch her children or her husband as they might have been in contact with a 'contaminated' object. The patient and her husband felt unhappy that they no longer had any physical contact and sexual intercourse was impossible. Helen could not touch her husband's pyjamas because they had been on the bathroom floor, nor could she touch her children, any clothing or object of theirs. Helen had an extensive course of behavioural treatment which eventually was very successful.

These cases of obsessive-compulsive disorder show how similar the condition is to a phobia: high anxiety is evident in both conditions and there is avoidance of situations which provoke this anxiety. The important difference between obsessive-compulsive disorders and phobias is that in obsessive-compulsive disorder the fear is not *of* the situations themselves but of their *consequences*. Also, elaborate belief systems develop around the rituals of obsessive-compulsive disorder, as Helen's case shows, but phobic people do not have these. Dirt phobia is really a misnomer and, as Helen's case indicated, she was really suffering from obsessive-compulsive disorder. The distinction is important because in obsessive-compulsive disorder the patient must learn to control the rituals and this often needs intensive treatment, often in hospital.

Temporal lobe epilepsy

'I keep having the feeling I have been here before'

Jane came for behavioural treatment because of long-standing panic attacks. These did not occur in any specific situation and she could get them just as easily sitting comfortably at home watching TV as she might walking along the street. Panic attacks of this kind respond to cognitive therapy where the patient is taught to cope with the overwhelming feelings of panic by using an alternative coping strategy such as relaxation exercises. Another approach is to look closely at the 'internal dialogue', which is what the patient says to herself.

It is common for patients to say to themselves unhelpful things such as 'I am sure I am going to die' or 'I am certain I will never survive this panic attack'. But the recurring thought Jane had was of a very different kind which she found extremely worrying. It was 'I have a feeling I have been here before.'

She described walking along a Cornish lane on holiday with her boyfriend. Suddenly she turned to him and said, 'I have this strange feeling I have walked along this lane before, but I don't know how I could have.'

Her boyfriend said there was nothing odd about her behaviour apart from this instance, but he told of how she kept on having these experiences. When they were travelling to the cinema by bus she became *convinced* that she had been on the *same* bus before. Not only the same number bus, but the *identical* bus at some time in the past. This feeling made her most uneasy.

Jane was experiencing what is known in medical jargon as *déjà vu*, often associated with a neurological condition called temporal lobe epilepsy. This is a kind of minor epilepsy where attacks are brought about by abnormal electrical activity over the temporal lobes of the cerebral cortex. Temporal lobe epilepsy can also produce panic attacks and the crucial test to prove the diagnosis is an electroencephalograph (EEG). I was eager to carry out this investigation but did not want to distress Jane further, who might not want to have this test. But she did seem very relieved with the outcome when the EEG showed abnormal spikes and sharp waves in the temporal lobes of her brain: 'I know now it's my brain and not my mind that has gone wrong.'

After referral to a neurologist colleague and appropriate anti-convulsant medication, the *déjà vu* and the panic attacks became things of the past.

Thyroid disorder

Father O'Donovan seemed a straightforward case of phobic disorder with panic attacks. He would panic before he had to speak in public which led to great difficulty carrying out his job as a priest. He had experienced no difficulty at the seminary and the problem started with his first church, gradually increasing over a two-year period. It had begun with anxiety during a service and he soon tried to avoid giving the sermon. Then he seemed anxious most of the time: 'I find myself trembling and shaking, pouring with sweat, and my legs feel as if I am going to collapse.'

My medical training makes me always consider the possibility of an organic disease in patients presenting with phobias. There was nothing about Father O'Donovan to suggest an organic disease, but I routinely run a screening test on phobic patients to check for over-activity of the thyroid gland, a condition called thyrotoxicosis. The result came back with one of the highest (abnormal) blood tests the lab had ever found. Referral to a physician specializing in endocrine disorders corrected the thyroid abnormality and most of Father O'Donovan's anxiety symptoms were brought under control.

Rare medical conditions

In addition to thyrotoxicosis there are various physical disorders such as hypoglycaemia (pathological lowering of the blood sugar) and phaeochromocytoma (a rare tumour causing over-activity of the adrenal gland) which sometimes should be tested for.

Substance-induced conditions must also be considered, including the common over-indulgence in tea or coffee which leads to caffeine-induced symptoms. (Some of these problems are

outlined in the case below.) Other stimulants such as ampheta-
mines can cause symptoms, as can withdrawal from barbiturates
and benzodiazepines.

Life-style problems

Donald, a 32-year-old unmarried merchant banker, was referred
to the clinic with a one-year history of severe panic episodes.
These could happen at any time of the day or night and
consisted of palpitations, sweating and a feeling of impending
doom. Each episode lasted for twenty-five to thirty minutes,
occurred four to six times a day, and Donald could not suggest
a reason or trigger for them. After getting the history of his
complaint, I asked about Donald's general life-style. He woke at
seven and left the house twenty minutes later, having had no
breakfast. A busy morning at work would mean drinking at
least three cups of fresh-ground coffee and lunch was a sandwich
or, if he was too busy, more frequently a bar of chocolate.
During the afternoon he would again have five to six cups of
coffee before finishing work at half past six or seven. He would
usually meet friends and eat in a restaurant, drinking up to a
bottle of wine, before returning home to bed after midnight. He
took little exercise and smoked about fifteen cigarettes a day.
Although he was not overweight, he had noticeably poor muscle
tone and terrible posture.

I explained to Donald that there were many factors in his life-
style which were probably contributing to his symptoms. Firstly,
his irregular meals could lead to hypoglycaemia (low blood
sugar) and by eating high carbohydrate food on an empty
stomach could lead to reactive hypoglycaemia. His smoking
habit and an excessive caffeine intake would both increase
stimulation to that part of his nervous system which controls
anxiety (the autonomic nervous system). The alcohol he drank
contributed to the problem by increasing his symptoms in the
morning and added to his morning hypoglycaemia. He worked
long hours in a sedentary job and his lack of fitness was
demonstrated by his resting pulse rate of 98/minute.

Clearly Donald could not alter his entire life-style immediately and I asked him what he felt able to tackle initially. He was sceptical that his life-style had any effect on his symptoms but eventually agreed to put this to the test and to eat three meals a day of the following foods. For breakfast he had a bowl of cornflakes and milk, for lunch a round of sandwiches (meat, fish or cheese), and a dinner of his choice in a restaurant. In addition, he agreed to stop drinking ground coffee and to change to the decaffeinated variety. I warned him that he could suffer from withdrawal symptoms, usually a headache, which can start twenty-four to forty-eight hours after the reduction in caffeine and can be accompanied by sweating and tremulousness. These symptoms should reduce after approximately twenty-four hours and Donald was asked to record his success and the time and situation of any panic episodes.

At the end of a week Donald reported that he was feeling much better than before. He had experienced a mild headache after reducing his intake of fresh coffee but this had settled quickly. Nearly all his funny turns were happening in the morning and he felt that he would like to reduce his alcohol intake to below the recommended limit of twenty-one units. He was advised on ways to pace and slow his drinking, as well as on low alcohol and alcohol-free beverages. Donald felt that he could reduce his alcohol intake best by travelling to the restaurant or pub in his car as he would never drink and drive. He could do this by refusing lifts from others and volunteering to take others in his car (over the past few years he felt that he owed most of his friends a large number of car journeys).

When Donald returned two weeks later, he had been remarkably successful in reducing his alcohol intake and he was only complaining of funny turns once or twice a week. He was then asked if he wanted to consolidate his gains for a while or to start another behavioural change. He felt that he did not want to cut down his smoking but asked about exercise. It was extremely important to find a form of exercise which he could enjoy regularly to increase his general fitness, reduce his heart rate and tendency to palpitations, but also to give him an interest apart from work. Indeed, regular aerobic exercise has been shown to have a beneficial effect on people with true anxiety symptoms.

Donald felt that he would hate jogging or running and, after some discussion, when Donald mentioned that he had been a member of the school swimming team, I suggested that he might like to visit the local baths to find out about life-saving classes, long-distance swimming clubs and clubs for adults. Donald agreed to the goal of going swimming at least three times a week.

Over the next few weeks he became increasingly enthusiastic about rediscovering swimming. He had joined a club for people over thirty which met twice a week and organized galas with races for different age groups. He had also managed to reduce his smoking and was planning to stop as he felt it had a deleterious effect on his swimming performance. The incidence of panic episodes was now negligible and this was still so when I saw him a year later.

This case, along with others, shows how easy it is to jump to the wrong conclusion that someone has a phobia. It also shows, however, that when a correct assessment has been made, there are many possible treatments for phobic-like symptoms, some of them medical and some of them involving life-style adjustments.

In brief

- Some cautionary tales to stop you jumping to the wrong conclusion that you have a phobia.
- Depression as an illness is commonly the cause of an unwillingness to go out and face people. This must not be confused with a phobia as it requires different and sometimes urgent treatment in its own right.
- Obsessive-compulsive disorder and so-called dirt phobia can seem very like true phobias but are quite distinct and require different treatment.
- Medical conditions such as some kinds of epilepsy, or an overactive thyroid gland and some rare medical conditions, can mimic phobias.
- Sometimes stress produces panic and phobia-like symptoms, and an alteration in life-style patterns can be helpful.
- Doctors have been known to be wrong, so do not be

surprised if your own self-assessment is wrong at first. Once the pitfalls are overcome, which might involve getting a professional opinion, self-therapy usually goes on to be very successful.

• Remember, if in any doubt about whether you really have a phobia, seek professional help.

8 The Role of Medication

'A miracle drug is any drug that will do what the label says it will do'

– E. Hodgins, 1889–1971

A 35-year-old woman with typical symptoms of agoraphobia said, 'Whatever else you do, I am not taking any more of those useless pills. My doctor started me off on Librium and then he changed it to Valium. Then I was drowsy all day, so I was switched to Ativan. They say on TV that these pills are addictive, so now I suppose I'm a drug addict as well as still being completely housebound.'

Many patients have pessimistic feelings about taking pills to help their phobias, while others of the opposite view think that a pill will solve all their problems.[1] The reality is somewhere in between: certain classes of medication can help some aspects of phobic disorders some of the time. The main classes of medication listed below show how this can be done.

Minor tranquillizers

With minor tranquillizers, of which diazepam (trade name Valium) is probably the most famous, we enter immediately a minefield of controversy. Some say that the combination of these drugs with behavioural therapy is a good idea as the two can benefit each other. Pills might also help by reducing the unpleasantness of the therapy. On the other hand, there may be harmful effects which operate by the mechanism of state-dependent learning. This occurs when learning takes place under the influence of drugs, including alcohol, and does not transfer to the non-drug state. An example of state-dependent learning involving alcohol could be those darts players who have learned to play well under the influence and who find that they cannot do so without alcohol. Others have suggested that drugs might impair the effectiveness of therapy by reducing tolerance to stress.

When you take a tablet, the effects can be quite complex. For instance, there is the so-called attribution effect where you face a phobic situation after taking a particular tablet, saying to yourself that you can only do so *because* of the drug. The effect of the drug may have been to boost your confidence through a psychological mechanism, although you attribute this to a pharmacological one.

Other truly pharmacological effects are tolerance and withdrawal. Tolerance means that increasingly larger amounts of medication have to be given to produce the same effect and this is a very real danger with the Valium type of drugs. Withdrawal effects occur with the same group of drugs and are the pharmacological effects of stopping them. One of the most important is the panic attacks that can be caused: clearly of great clinical relevance given that these are often the problem presented in the first place!

In a controlled study diazepam given in moderate doses just before facing the feared situation made no difference to the outcome, but in regular doses was better than a beta-blocker drug (see below). Some therapists believe that failure to improve is often related to taking large amounts of benzodiazepines or alcohol. Despite this, in my experience, *some* people are helped to overcome avoidance by small doses of diazepam.

'I will never get on that underground train unless I can take 5mg of Valium just before,' stated a 24-year-old woman who had, for no apparent reason, developed a fear of travelling on the underground two years earlier. She worked in the City of London and had to use this particular transport every day, despite the discomfort it caused her. She had no avoidance as long as she took the Valium tablet, which she had considered taking for ever until her own doctor put her under pressure to stop doing so.

The tablet may have a direct anxiety-reducing effect which

makes it easier to cope with the feared situation. In addition, there is a strong psychological effect: each time this patient took it she expected to feel better and this expectation was reinforced each time she did and she *did* feel better. The problem of treatment was that if she ventured into the feared situation without medication she would *expect* to feel worse.

She was motivated to come off medication because of her fear of remaining on it for ever. She was persuaded to do the necessary homework exercises of gradually going out more and more to face her feared situation, but she would only agree to do so with some medication. The dose was therefore reduced – initially to 2mg for one week, then 1mg for one week – so that eventually she was able to travel without taking any medication at all. She still insisted on carrying a small supply of 1mg tablets in her handbag, but had not actually taken any of them when she saw me at follow-up a year later. What had happened could possibly be explained in terms of the safety signal theory which states that a small amount of medication becomes conditioned to 'safety', with the tablets no longer necessary for the pharmacological action they originally had.

Antidepressant medication

'But I'm not depressed, Doctor' is a well-known plea when this treatment is suggested to most phobic patients. The use of these drugs goes back to 1964 when the New York psychiatrist Donald Klein suggested that imipramine might lower anxiety in agoraphobia. His research team reported that imipramine was superior to a placebo (a dummy drug capsule containing no active ingredient) in both agoraphobic and mixed phobic groups but not in simple phobics. In that study two kinds of psychological treatment were also compared in patients receiving either a drug or a placebo. The combination of supportive psychotherapy and imipramine was slightly superior to the combination of an early form of behaviour therapy called desensitization in fantasy and imipramine. (We now consider desensitization in fantasy to be a very weak treatment.) Another problem that has made interpretation difficult for this and similar studies is that patients may obtain self-exposure in uncontrolled ways because it becomes that 'self-exposure makes you better' when you attend a phobia clinic. There have been ten subsequent studies of imipramine, making it the most widely studied drug. The size of the drug effect is unclear and it has a delayed onset as might be expected. Exposure therapy facilitates the effect of imipramine, but it could also be that imipramine facilitates the effect of exposure.

To pursue this question, a large study was carried out in the USA which randomly assigned thirty-seven severely disabled agoraphobic patients to: a group receiving imipramine and no exposure; a group receiving imipramine *plus* exposure; a placebo plus exposure group. For a more stringent test of the pharmacological effects of imipramine independent of exposure to phobic stimuli, patients in the first group received anti-exposure instructions during the first eight weeks of therapy. At eight weeks, the second group receiving imipramine combined with exposure therapy showed more improvement than the other two groups, and was the only one to show a reduction in panic attacks.

In my clinical practice I combine exposure therapy with imipramine when the patient lacks confidence to venture into the feared situation and suffers from panic attacks, recognizing that many patients are fearful of medication or cannot tolerate the drug's side-effects. But some cases do benefit and, as one of my patients put it, 'The ideas you suggested are all very well but I can never go into the supermarket because of the state I get into outside. I tremble, shake and sweat so much, I just have to go home in the end, even though I know I should go inside.'

This patient was put on imipramine, starting with 25mg daily for a week, increasing by 25mg increments each week until she was taking 75mg at the end of the third week. She found that the panic attacks were less severe then and she could continue with behavioural therapy. She remained on 75mg imipramine for a three-month period, after which it was withdrawn and she remained free of phobic symptoms a year later.

There have been studies of other antidepressant drugs and the one of clomipramine suggests that it is also of value in combination with exposure therapy. In 1980 a research team at the Maudsley Hospital investigated the effect of combining clomipramine and behavioural therapy in obsessive-compulsive disorder. We found that clomipramine was definitely of value and many have supported its use in phobias, although whether it is any better or worse than imipramine remains unknown.

Another category of antidepressant is the so-called mono-amine-oxidase-inhibitor, of which the most widely used in phobias is phenelzine (trade name Nardil). This category of drug achieved notoriety in the 1960s when it was discovered that if you ate cheese with it you were likely to suffer a sudden rise in blood pressure which could lead to a stroke or even death. But some controlled studies show the beneficial effects of this class of drug. For example, a study in the UK of forty outpatients with either social phobia or agoraphobia showed the superiority of phenelzine to a placebo. Each group was carefully matched for type of phobia, duration of phobia, depression, sex and overall severity. A flexible dose regime was used with all patients starting on one tablet (15mg) daily, increasing to 45mg daily after a week. As patients were encouraged to test themselves in the phobic situations, this could have improved the overall results.

Nowadays, because of the dangers of food and drug interactions with this class of drug, it is less likely to be used. This has become even more true recently with the advent of the 5-HT uptake inhibitor class of drug, for example, paroxetine (trade name Seroxat). These drugs are also known as the SSRI class (Specific Serotonin Re-uptake Inhibitor). Other SSRI drugs are fluoxetine (Prozac), fluvoxamine (Faverin) and sertraline (Lustral). They are known informally among psychiatrists as 'miracle drugs', which of course they are not. They do, however, seem free of some of the unwanted side-effects like dry mouth and constipation experienced with imipramine and clomipramine. However, to date, controlled trials in phobic disorders are still awaited with the SSRI drugs.

Beta-blocker drugs

Beta-blockers were developed to control high blood pressure, and then found to have a useful effect in slowing down nervous activity raised in anxiety. A particular kind of receptor in the nervous system, the beta-receptor, is responsible for this kind of activity. When beta-reception is blocked, certain symptoms of anxiety are reduced: these include shakiness of the hands, palpitations of the heart and over-reaction of the bowel.

There are conflicting studies in the research on this area. For instance one study found beta-blockers were superior to a placebo when given along with exposure therapy, but another found beta-blockers inferior to diazepam. Beta-blockers in moderate doses have no central effects on the nervous system, so the mode of action depends on the peripheral blockade of the sympathetically mediated mechanisms underlying the symptom. Bodily symptoms may reinforce anxiety and so a vicious cycle can be set up. Therefore, for patients in whom tremor, palpitations or diarrhoea are the major symptoms, beta-blockers can play an important role combining with the cognitive therapy for anxiety states. As with all medication, the treatment has to be weighed against the side-effects, relatively few with this class of drug but some patients experience faintness which they can find difficult to bear. The dosage of medication has to be tailored to the individual patient: for example, propranalol is often begun at 10mg daily and increased gradually to 120mg daily.

Conclusions

It is fair to say that despite the great advances made in drug therapy in the last forty years, there is no drug answer to solve the problem of phobias. How could there be, you might say, when phobias are so varied and people's responses so complex. On the other hand, there is probably no need to throw out the baby with the bath water and ignore medication. A single dose of a tranquillizer, even the dreaded Valium, has made all the difference to progress in some of my patients. Remember that Valium can take up to thirty minutes to begin to work, so you will need to allow for this before facing the situation you have been avoiding. You may also have to experiment as the exact time varies from person to person. Remember also that tranquillizers can make you drowsy, so you should not drive under their influence. Their effects are often made stronger by alcohol, 'the oldest tranquillizer known to man'. It is worth emphasizing that there are grave dangers of one drink leading to another with a great risk of becoming dependent on alcohol. For this reason it is not a good idea to use alcohol as your tranquillizer.

It is worth remembering that there is more than one category of medication and not all pills are the same. It is fine to take one tablet of Valium but absolutely useless to do so with anti-depressants. Here it is crucial to have a certain concentration of the medication in your blood all the time, so you must take a course of the medication, rather as you do a course of antibiotics. Your doctor will advise you about the dose and how long it should be taken. The regime for the beta-blockers is somewhat in between: in some cases one or two doses may be helpful just before facing stress, but often it is best to have a course of these tablets. There is no danger of becoming addicted to beta-blockers or most antidepressants.

It might be difficult at first to appreciate that such different classes of medication as antidepressants and tranquillizers can both be helpful in treating phobias – but in their own way. The tranquillizers damp down anxiety and *can* be useful to help someone with a phobia face the situation for the first time. The treatment plan with tranquillizers would be to reduce the dose as soon as the patient's confidence increases and then carry on the treatment without medication. Antidepressants work in a completely different way: they affect transmission of electrical messages in certain parts of the brain. This helps to reduce panic attacks and may make behavioural treatment easier. A course of treatment with antidepressants is often for several months.

In brief

- If you were determined never to take tablets, you might just change your mind. There is evidence that some tablets do help some people some of the time.
- Not all tablets are the same and, in particular, antidepres-sants are very different from tranquillizers. The former are not addictive but the latter can be.

- Small doses of an antidepressant are often helpful with anxiety or phobias.
- A third category of medication known as beta-blockers is used to lower blood pressure but is also helpful for the specific anxiety symptoms of tremor, palpitations and diarrhoea.
- On the whole it is best to avoid self-medication with that ancient tranquillizer known as alcohol.

9 Self-Help

> 'The physician becomes a therapeutic figure for
> the patient, whatever he says, whatever he does.
> He may see the patient once, a dozen times, or (if
> he is a psychiatrist) a thousand times. He may
> provide advice, support, or analysis, but whatever
> he elects to do, his relationship to the patient is
> pre-eminent. His authority, his sympathy, and the
> countless intangible and largely unconscious
> bonds which are forged in an effective doctor–
> patient relationship are as important as the sense
> or otherwise of anything he says and does'
>
> – Oliver Sacks, 1970

Despite the truth of Oliver Sacks's quotation many people will
want to try to help themselves overcome a phobia. This chapter
is for those who, for whatever reason, *cannot* receive specialist
psychiatric help. If you have read so far, but still feel confused,
it may be of help to you. It starts with a flow chart, a kind of
road map, to guide you to relevant chapters.

People are anxious for all kinds of reasons. You may have a
physical disorder rather similar to one of those described in
chapter 7 'Misconceptions'. The flow chart is a way of helping
you solve problems by giving a yes or no answer to a series of
questions:

Q.1 Do you think you might have a physical disorder
similar to one of those described in chapter 7?
If your answer is yes, then go to the doctor. You might
help your doctor by finding out if there is a family
history of thyroid disorders or of epilepsy. You could
also think about your intake of caffeine-containing

drinks, as well as other life-style details, and keep a
record of these.
If your answer is no, proceed to *Q.2*.

Q.2 Do you have problems about leaving the house, being
in open spaces or going on public transport? Are your
problems similar to those described in chapter 2
'Agoraphobia'?
If your answer is yes, fill in the following
questionnaire. This will give you a rough idea of how
serious your phobia is.
If your answer is no, proceed to *Q.3*.

AGORAPHOBIA QUESTIONNAIRE
0   1   2   3   4   5   6   7   8
A score of 0 means no difficulty and a score of 8 means
impossible to do. The numbers in between represent the
degree of difficulty the activity has for you.

Score
- [ ] Walking alone in a busy street
- [ ] Going into crowded shops
- [ ] Venturing out into large open spaces
- [ ] Travelling alone on public transport
- [ ] Going alone far from home
- [ ] *Total score*

If your total score is 10, then you have mild
agoraphobia, 20 moderate agoraphobia and 40 severe
agoraphobia. Now you know about the severity of the
agoraphobia, follow the self-help lines (Self-help for
agoraphobia p.119), depending upon whether you have a
partner (or a helpful friend) who can assist.

Q.3 Do you have problems in social situations similar to
those described in chapter 3 'Social Phobias'?
If your answer is yes, fill in the following social
phobia questionnaire.
If your answer is no, proceed to *Q.4*.

SOCIAL PHOBIA QUESTIONNAIRE
0   1   2   3   4   5   6   7   8
A score of 0 means no difficulty and a score of 8 means
impossible to do. The numbers in between represent the
degree of difficulty the activity has for you.

Score
- ☐ Being with people you do not know very well
- ☐ Making the first move starting up a friendship
- ☐ Talking to people in authority
- ☐ Eating in front of other people
- ☐ Going into a room full of other people
- ☐ *Total score*

If your total score is 10, then you have mild social
phobia, 20 moderate and 40 severe social phobia. Now you
know about the severity of the social phobia, try to
determine which of the three types of social phobia
applies in your case and follow the treatment lines
suggested.

The three kinds are: a) lack of social skills (see
                        p.130);
                     b) lack of assertiveness (see
                        p.131);
                     c) lack of impulse control (see
                        p.132).

Q.4 Do you have fear and avoidance of other specific
situations?
If your answer is yes, read chapters 4 'Animal Phobia'
and 5 'Various Phobias' to try to find a case similar to
your own and fill in the specific phobia questionnaire
below:
If no, proceed to *Q.5*.

SPECIFIC PHOBIA QUESTIONNAIRE
Here you will have to improvise a little as it will
depend on exactly what it is that you are phobic of. The
important thing is to distinguish between *dislike* of

something which can be perfectly normal and a true phobia
for which you may decide you need treatment. Write your
phobia in the blank spaces.

-------- prevents me doing what I want in life
-------- stops me enjoying holidays anywhere
-------- makes me anxious when I am near it
-------- stops me making a career move
-------- makes me feel constant tension

0 1 2 3 4 5 6 7 8
A score of 0 means never and a score of 8 means all the
time. The numbers in between represent the severity the
activity has for you.

If your score is 10 you have a mild phobia, 20 a moderate
phobia and 40 a severe phobia.

Q.5 Are your fears to do with your sex life?
If your answer is yes, then read chapter 6 'Sexual
Phobias' which outlines the main sexual fears for men and
women. For men: difficulty with erections, premature
ejaculation or failure of ejaculation. For women: painful
or impossible sexual intercourse, problems of orgasm.
Follow the appropriate treatment lines for your
particular case.

Self-help for agoraphobia

One common problem for people with agoraphobia getting help
is that they cannot leave the house. Or it could be that specialist
help is not available in your area, or that a waiting-list is many
months long. This is a self-help section and chapter 8 'The Role
of Medication' tells you what can be obtained from your general
practitioner to help with phobic problems.

First, find out whether you do have a phobia, what type it is,
and how bad it is. The simple questionnaires above are to help
you with this and, afterwards, it would be a good idea to
read again the description of appropriate cases where professional help was given (for example, 'The girl who could not
go out').

When you have done this, it is time to rehearse the three golden rules:

- Anxiety is unpleasant but it does no harm
- As you face anxiety, the level of anxiety lessens over time
- Practice makes perfect.

Think about what practical steps you can take to begin to treat yourself. Let us first of all consider how each rule could apply to you.

Anxiety is unpleasant but it does no harm

People often think they are going to die in an anxiety attack. This is because the symptoms are so unpleasant and make you feel very uncomfortable: sweating, dry mouth, breathlessness, palpitations, etcetera. One way of proving that you will not die is to do some physical exercise to bring on these symptoms. Mild exercise such as running on the spot for ten minutes gives many people some of the above symptoms. On the whole, physically fit people do not die from mild physical exercise. Another way to try to prove to yourself that anxiety does no harm is to consider the normal anxiety anybody would expect to feel in a genuinely fearful situation. To do this, imagine the following scene:

A tiger has escaped from the zoo and appears outside your window. As you turn to look at it, the tiger bounds through the window, shattering the glass, and it lands on a table in front of you. It places its huge paw on your chest and pushes you to the ground. The tiger stands over you with its jaws open a few inches from your face. You hear the tiger roar and feel the animal's teeth sink into your flesh . . .

The idea is for you to continue imagining this scene to see if you can bring on symptoms. If you succeed, then carry on until the symptoms lessen. How successful you are may depend upon your ability to create and sustain visual imagery. In any event remember the point of the exercise: real tigers can harm you but imaginary ones cannot. The phobic situation is similar to a real tiger for you, but it is a way of proving that anxiety in itself does no harm.

As you face anxiety, the level of anxiety lessens over time
The principle here is habituation, referred to throughout. An everyday example may serve to illustrate habituation: if you have a cat or a dog, try the effect of giving it a repeated stimulus. For example, touch your cat lightly on the ear. It will probably move its whole head towards you the first time. The second time you touch it, perhaps it will only move its ear. The third time there will be only the smallest movement of its ear and, finally, depending on your cat, probably no movement at all. Habituation to anxiety occurs in a similar way and this has important practical applications when you try to overcome your phobia: time and time again I hear from patients who have not *persisted* in staying for long enough in the phobic situation to allow habituation:

'I thought I was really good last week. For the first time in months I forced myself to go to the shops. Everything was fine for the first five minutes. Then I had a terrible feeling of fear. I started to sweat and had the butterflies in my tummy kind of feeling. That is it, I thought. I'm not putting up with this. I ran outside and hailed a taxi to take me straight home. I felt better as soon as I left the shop, better still inside the taxi and best of all when I arrived home.'

This account was from a woman with typical symptoms of agoraphobia who was *maintaining* her symptoms by never spending long enough in the phobic situation. Another way of seeing how she made herself worse was to consider how avoidance was being clearly rewarded (or reinforced). Every time she ran away, she felt better. Running away became conditioned to feeling better. Running away was increasingly likely to happen as time went on.

Practice makes perfect
Learning to overcome anxiety is as hard as any other kind of learning. You are trying to break patterns of conditioning built up over years. Try to think of an example of where you tried to learn something difficult in everyday life. Did learning to drive or learning to type come easily to you? How much practice did you have to put in? The unlearning of a phobia could be seen as a special kind of learning because you are having to break

established patterns of behaviour. Can you remember having to unlearn something such as learning to use a different typewriter keyboard or learning to drive on the other side of the road? Old habits die hard.

Practical steps

If you have agoraphobia, then sooner or later you will have to work out a way of facing the outside world again. Using self-therapy may be slower than getting professional help but the principles are similar: push yourself to go into the phobic situation as fast as you reasonably can, but do not go out just briefly and frighten yourself. One of my patients made the following list of steps to overcome thirty-five years' agoraphobia:

1 Open the front door and walk to the garden gate (about 20 yards) with the garden gate shut
2 Open the garden gate
3 Walk to the postbox at the corner of street (about 50 yards from the gate) with your dog
4 Walk to the corner shop (about 100 yards) with your dog
5 Go into the corner shop with your dog
6 Repeat 3 to 5 without your dog
7 Go to the shopping precinct to larger shops.

You could attempt a similar list tailor-made to your own particular problem and set aside a short time every day to practise. Begin with the easiest item on the list but, if you feel it is too easy, try a step further down. It is important to try walking towards the postbox *every* day, even if you do not make it there at first. The crucial thing is that you are getting into the habit of trying to get to the postbox.

Once you have succeeded at a task, repeat it several times. It could be that you just had a lucky day! You need to persuade yourself that it gets easier each time and that it was *not* just luck. The only way to convince yourself is to keep on having success: nothing succeeds like success! When you are consistently successful with one item, then, and only then, proceed to the next task on your list.

What can you do if progress stops and, however hard you try, you cannot reach the next item? It could be that the step to the next item is too demanding: after walking to the postbox (50 yards), you might find going to the corner shop (100 yards) too difficult. If this is the case, try to find somewhere between these points that could act as an intermediate step. Do not worry if there is no actual landmark at that distance. The important thing to remember is that intermediate steps will probably enable you to achieve a worthwhile step later on.

If this intermediate step is still too hard, then try the relaxation exercises described on p.139 and read about self-cognitive therapy. If both of these fail, you might like to consider asking your doctor for some medication described in chapter 8. But remember that the medication is to *assist* you to face the task. It will not do it for you and any progress will be a result of the effort you make yourself.

The use of cognitive self-therapy
'Neurosis essentially seems to consist of stupid behaviour by non-stupid people'

– Albert Ellis, 1962

People with phobias and other neurotic difficulties are often told to pull themselves together and, in my experience, this does no good at all. What can help, however, is to think about what you say to yourself and whether this is 'stupid behaviour', in the sense of it being an unhelpful or unconstructive way of dealing with the problem. For example, you may feel a little faint when walking along the street and say to yourself: 'I feel faint. That means I am about to collapse. I shall probably lose control any minute and make a fool of myself. Perhaps I shall have a heart attack or even die.'

It is obvious that this kind of self-talk is not exactly helpful. It is what cognitive therapists call magnifying the symptoms and the antidote is to try to test out each of the ideas to yourself to prove that the probability of them happening is rather low. Let us take each idea in turn:

1 *I feel faint*

This is a genuine feeling and there is nothing necessarily wrong with it. Perfectly fit and normal people feel faint now and again. If you do not believe this, try to gather some evidence by asking your friends. When one of my patients did so, she was suitably impressed to discover that a friend who had won prizes for physical fitness at a local aerobics club also experienced faintness from time to time. This helped persuade her that feeling faint could be quite normal. Another patient, a man who had served in the army, recalled how fit soldiers often fainted on parade and this helped him to accept that fainting was not terribly serious.

2 *I shall . . . make a fool of myself*

Patients with agoraphobia often feel they will become the centre of attention in a panic attack and this leads them to avoid going out. Try to ask yourself exactly *how* you think you will make a fool of yourself in public. When a 20-year-old woman asked herself this, she wrote in her diary: 'I will probably fall to the ground . . . Everybody will crowd round me . . . Perhaps I will wet myself . . . People will stare at me and I will lose control . . . Perhaps I will have a fit.'

She was a perfectly healthy young woman with no history of epilepsy or urinary disorder. In her mind she was building up, out of all proportion, what had a very slight probability of happening. When I saw her ten years ago I asked her to write the fears out using the two-column method described in detail in chapter 2. This is what she wrote:

I will fall down	This is very unlikely as I have never done so
I will wet myself	As I have never wet myself, I am unlikely to start now
I will have a fit	I have no history of epilepsy and there is no epilepsy in my family

She carried these cards in her handbag and from them got the courage to face the outside world. When I saw her recently (ten years after that first consultation), she still had the original cards in her handbag. They were dog-eared, with the ink faded and smudged, but they still retained the power to enable her to face the outside world.

3 *I shall have a heart attack or even die*

This was exactly what George said to himself. The story of how he cured himself is worth telling as others may be able to help themselves too. George was forty-five years old and had lived with his phobia of driving in traffic for twenty years. He was a tough, cheerful Cockney who had overcome years of considerable childhood deprivation and had been brought up in a Dr Barnado's Home. He lived in the rugged world of roofers and thought nothing of going up a ladder in heavy rain to replace roof tiles on London houses. He had recently set up his own roofing business and this meant driving around London to give estimates to potential customers. Because of the phobia he was losing money: the London traffic was too bad for him to cope with other than on Sunday mornings or before six in the morning on weekdays.

'I dread being stuck in traffic and having a heart attack, even though I know this is bloody stupid. I am determined not to let my business go down the drain after all the hard work I have put in to build it up . . .

'I said to myself, Suppose I could *prove* that I wouldn't have a heart attack or at least that this would be unlikely. Then, perhaps, I could get the bottle to face the traffic in my car.

'So then I thought I would go for one of those medical screenings where they do ECGs and all that. Of course the result showed damn all wrong with my heart. Just as I thought it would . . .

'Next, I worked out that the only way to get over the phobia was to treat it like going up a ladder – bloody well force myself to face it and tell myself at the same time that the medical tests had proved that my heart was OK. So I started driving in traffic. Every time I thought I was getting a heart pain, I said to myself this is just anxiety. Keep going and the anxiety will pass. My heart must be OK. Keep going to prove that anxiety does pass. The tests show there is nothing wrong with my bloody heart. If I keep practising this, it will be as easy as going up the stairs.

George showed great courage. He came to tell me his story because he had heard from a friend of my interest in phobias and wanted to know if I was interested in what he called 'a bloody miracle cure'. I certainly *was* and promised to pass on his story. He is now running a very successful roofing company.

A question patients often ask is, 'What will I be left with if you take away my phobia? Will something worse take its place?' George's story may reassure patients: his life became fuller, he is a happier person and nothing terrible did replace his phobia. Planning for the future should be an important part of your treatment for, as the agoraphobia diminishes, you can do what you could never have envisaged. Now is the time to visit your long-suffering friends who once had to visit you. Now is the time to join that aerobics class, or the one on car maintenance you always fancied but could never get to before. The ultimate aid in raising self-esteem for many agoraphobic patients is to get a job and many have done just this.

The role of the partner of an agoraphobic

The cases of Jill and June show how crucial it is to involve the partner of a patient with agoraphobia. This is more likely to be a man, so I shall refer to *him*, but it could, of course, be a woman who is the partner of a sufferer. The first thing is to recognize *why* your help is so crucial: you probably know your partner better than anyone and so are in an ideal position to help. You are also the person at home where all the practice will begin.

Giving the right kind of help is important and it is all too common for the partner to trip up over his own kindness here. Most partners of agoraphobic women I meet are caring and concerned men who cannot bear to see how their partners are suffering. They lean over backwards to do the shopping, collect the children from school and drive their partner everywhere she wants to go. This is the trouble! It is important to learn how to encourage your partner to become independent of you and it is no easy task if you remain convinced yourself that something terrible will happen to her if you are not at her side. One of my patients' partner recently told me that he thought she would die of a heart attack during an anxiety episode, although she was a perfectly fit woman. Persuading him that his belief was mistaken was clearly important before he could help his partner. Encouraging her to go out on her own is the key to helping your partner overcome agoraphobia.

The encouragement you give may not at first lead to success. If it does, you should encourage her to try again and to go further afield. Where partners usually run into problems is when the sufferer has an initial failure which can be depressing for both of you. A useful trick here is to try a smaller step forward, not something so easy that she can do it already but an easier task than at first. Regular practise in small stages which achieve success is preferable to trying too much and failing.

Another problem for partners is how to cope with a panic attack. In the first place do not panic yourself, though for some men this is easier said than done. The key to dealing with panics is to remember the golden rules, and to try by any means to prevent your partner leaving the situation until the panic has subsided. 'I couldn't be such a sadist as to stay there and watch her suffer' was the response of one of my patients' partner. I explained to him that he did not have to just watch. Try to talk to your partner in a calm way, at the same time reminding her of the importance of remaining in the situation. There may be certain tricks you can use to help with specific symptoms. For example, for hyperventilation (breathing too fast), you could encourage your partner to breathe into a paper bag. This technique helps with the reabsorption of carbon dioxide that can be a problem with over-rapid breathing. Taking slow, easy breaths can also help the symptoms of nausea as can going through some of the relaxation exercises. So you do not have to think of yourself as sadistic: you are *helping* your partner overcome agoraphobia.

It is not uncommon to see couples caught in a trap of the man becoming increasingly critical of his partner, who feels resentful and despondent. It is hardly surprising that no progress is made in this situation. If you see this happening, try to be less critical and look for some way to give praise instead. Your partner will become more cheerful and more likely to carry out practice in facing a feared situation if you are encouraging. One of my patients loved to be taken out to a restaurant but, of course, had to be driven to the door each time. After a while she agreed to her partner's idea of parking the car a few hundred yards away from the restaurant and, eventually, in the next block. This may sound a bit like bribery but it did enable the couple to break the cycle of criticism.

The family car can be the focus of much agoraphobic tension for although patients with agoraphobia usually can drive themselves, only a few feel safe when driven by others. Getting a car might mean that you never need to overcome phobic avoidance of public transport, but on the other hand many agoraphobics' lives are transformed for the better when they learn to drive. The pros and cons will have to be worked out for your particular situation and will depend on your income and whether good public transport is available locally.

The question of holidays is of special significance in agoraphobia. As treatment becomes progressively more successful, agoraphobics are usually able to go on longer car trips or on train journeys and then, usually last of all, travel by aeroplane. Holidays clearly need careful planning and negotiating if they are to be fun and also relaxing. Being a psychiatric nurse for two weeks in Spain, while your partner recovers from the outward journey and anticipates the return, is not advisable. But taking advantage of successes and making sure that the holiday is rewarding to you both should be the objective.

Even if you decide not to seek professional help, remember that you are not alone having an agoraphobic partner. It is often a great support to join one of the self-help groups for relatives and sufferers listed under Advice Sources.

In brief
- Anxiety is unpleasant but it does no harm.
- As you confront anxiety, the level of anxiety lessens.

- Practice makes perfect.
- Use the two-column technique to teach yourself encouraging reminders.
- The role of your partner is important.
- Try specific techniques such as relaxation and breathing help with panic attacks.
- Praise from a partner is better than criticism.
- Use a car, if this is helpful.
- You are not alone with agoraphobia: join a self-help group.

Self-help for social phobias

You may identify with some of my socially phobic patients. To help yourself, you will need to decide whether it is a true phobia (an irrational fear of a situation) or simply whether you lack the necessary skills to cope with a social situation. Agoraphobia and social phobias almost merge in some people, so it is hardly surprising that their treatment is similar. In the first instance, the self-help approach involves learning to face up to the situation, using the three golden rules. Remember that the key to a phobia is fear and avoidance of a specific situation: a socially phobic young man felt hot and self-conscious especially when he thought people were looking at him. He avoided eating in his works canteen and could not celebrate his eldest sister's wedding. I set him the homework exercise of going to lunch in his canteen even if he felt people were looking at him. In this way he gradually overcame his problem and, gaining in confidence, he attended his youngest sister's wedding some years later. For your own situation, pinpoint what you avoid. Then work out a way to face it, without giving in to avoidance. Remember, anxiety is unpleasant but it does no harm. You will have to face it more than once as practice makes perfect. As you stay in the phobic situation, the anxiety will lessen: anxiety does eventually lessen.

With people who lack social skills it may be that they have to learn to stand up for themselves (as in Jeffrey's case) or that they lack proper control of their impulses and are afraid of hitting out or becoming violent. These problems are so clearly opposite sides of a coin that you should have no difficulty determining which category you fall into.

Lack of social skills

Social skills are similar to many other skills: they can be learned by copying others with these skills. Most people learn them as they grow up but some do not. This missed opportunity can be made up later on by extra tuition. If you did not socialize as a child, it could help to join a club of some sort. This might be an evening class where you have the opportunity to relate to others or a drama club where the 'rules' of how to present yourself confidently can be acquired. Some of these rules are:

Use an expressive tone. Listen to how other people talk and try to imitate them. Make a tape-recording of yourself or, better still, a video-recording and play it back. On play-back you may become aware of what it is you are doing wrong. Now is your chance to correct this without anyone knowing. Speaking faster, more fluently and with more powerful emphasis can all be practised. As well as the words you use, look at what psychologists call non-verbal behaviour: the way you hold your body and what you do with your hands. Men commonly make the mistake of keeping their hands awkwardly in their pockets and women tug at their clothing. For practice, imagine that you are going for a job interview: think up some questions that you could be asked and make a tape of yourself answering these.

Also worth practising are the rules of eye contact. On first meeting someone it is usual to make brief eye contact and it is useful to do so when making a point. Direct eye contact is usually broken off and then resumed briefly during conversation. Brief eye contact is normally made on parting.

In social situations alcohol is a time-honoured social lubricant but a word of warning may be useful. One drink may be helpful but if one leads to two, and so on, then this is clearly not going to be the case. I have seen patients who began as social phobics and ended up alcohol-dependent. Do not fool yourself into thinking that you perform better after several drinks: when this experiment was carried out with London bus drivers there was conclusive proof that their driving became worse, although they thought it was getting better.

Lack of assertiveness

Have you had poor service in a restaurant but been too shy to complain? Do you feel that people push in front of you in queues but you do nothing about it? Do others always make more of an impression at your workplace or in social situations? If your answer is yes, then what follows is for you.

Lack of assertiveness means not being able to do what you want to do in the appropriate social situation. But I am not suggesting that you do what you want in *all* situations. Telling your boss what you think of him could be a quick way of getting fired. On the other hand, putting in for a rise at the appropriate time and place could be properly assertive behaviour.

Our personalities are shaped by the conditioning at work since we were born. It is not surprising that it might be a hard job undoing all that. As folklore puts it, you can't teach an old dog new tricks. But human behaviour *is* changeable and if you set your mind to it you can learn more assertive behaviour. Another saying is that nothing succeeds like success and I am going to suggest exercises for some positive success experiences to give you confidence to gradually build up a repertoire of assertive behaviour to use in daily life. Do not worry if at first these ideas seem a little extreme.

A good starting-point is the following exercise. Go up to a stranger in the street and ask for directions. You can choose someone who looks friendly and helpful, and it does not matter that you are not really lost. The main aim here is to get a positive response so that you will be encouraged.

The next exercise is one I have often suggested. Go to an expensive car showroom and ask for a test drive. Most patients go to their local dealer and tell me that they just could not see themselves test-driving an expensive foreign car. This does not really matter as the point of the exercise is to practise asserting yourself and to have positive, success experiences.

The third exercise may sound very embarrassing but people

who succeed have found it most helpful. Go into a chemist's shop and ask for a packet of condoms in a loud, clear voice. One step further is to ask for a discount for buying a large supply!

The final exercise is to go into a private art gallery and ask to look round, something most gallery owners will encourage. The next step is to make detailed inquiries about buying a particular picture. Then say that you have changed your mind.

These exercises should be seen only as examples. If you think they are too silly or impossible for you to perform, then make up your own assertion exercises. Remember the basic principle is for you to do something you thought you could not do and have a success experience.

Lack of impulse control

Some people seem to have the proverbial short fuse and lose their tempers at the least provocation. This can get them into problems with their relationships and in extreme cases can mean that they end up in gaol.

One apparently friendly young man could not stop hitting people. He usually did this on a Saturday night after a few drinks when he would get into an argument and hit out at the person with whom he disagreed. Once he punched a friend on the jaw and his friend's head banged against the wall behind, leaving him unconscious for some minutes. This really frightened my patient and he asked for help.

One suggestion was to point out the link between his short fuse and his drinking. This clarified but did not solve the problem. What finally did help was for him to rehearse in his mind's eye what *might* happen if he hit someone. This worst-case scenario followed:

I see this bloke in the pub on a Saturday night and we have this row. I hit him on the jaw and his head goes back against the wall with a thud. He slumps to the ground and does not get up. Blood trickles out of the corner of his mouth. The ambulance is called and they try to revive him. They give up and take the body away. The police come and put the handcuffs on me. I am taken away in a police van. I appear in court and the judge gives me a severe sentence. My name is in all the newspapers. My parents are ashamed of me and I have nowhere to live when I leave prison. All my friends are ashamed of me.

The patient wrote this down and he reminded himself of it whenever he had the urge to hit someone. If you have a similar problem, work out your own worst-case scenario script with relevance to your situation. Then start to think it to yourself, rather like running a film in your head. The start of the 'film' should be as soon as you recognize the risk of your harmful behaviour.

In brief

- Set objectives which must be both possible and realistic.
- Break down your problem into smaller manageable components which will be easy to tackle.
- Consider self-expression: follow the exercises to develop it.
- Become aware of your effect on other people and collect information about this so that you can change your behaviour.

Lack of social skills
- Understand other people's intentions.
- Learn to use an expressive tone from role models. Make tape-recordings to provide feedback.
- Learn to speak fluently: use an audio-cassette or, better still, a video-recorder for feedback.
- Speak faster (also using tape).
- Use powerful speech (also using tape).
- Non-verbal behaviour: use a mirror or, best of all, a video-taped feedback.
- Use the rules of eye contact.
- Remember the problem of alcohol or other recreational drugs as social lubricants. Mostly this is not a good idea.

Lack of assertion
- Self-assertion: learn when to use it to stand up for yourself and also when it might be inadvisable.

Lack of impulse control

- Lack of impulse control can be dealt with by anger management, a group of techniques directed at training recognition of early cues that trigger the impulse.

Self-help for specific phobias

In the cases of patients with specific phobias you may have come across a case-history similar to your own. Some needed many hours of therapy because they were often complex cases referred to a specialist clinic. Many common phobias of animals and of specific situations can be relatively easy to treat yourself. Self-help for a specific phobia *can* be easier than it is for agoraphobia or social phobia. This is because it is simpler to arrange contact with, for example, a dog or a cat. However, other situations like thunderstorms are more difficult to arrange to order! What you have to decide is whether you really want to overcome your phobia. This may seem obvious but it is easy to fool yourself. The acid test is to ask yourself how much you would stand to gain by losing the phobia. (The spider-phobic patient I have described really needed to overcome his phobia so that he could put his precious motor cycle away in the garden shed.) Ask yourself: What will I gain if I overcome the phobia? Then ask yourself: Am I prepared to put up with some discomfort at first to get over my phobia? Only proceed with self-help if your answers to both questions are positive.

The next stage is to draw up a step-by-step plan of dealing with the behaviour you want to change. We can call this an action plan. Then you should draw up a plan to deal with unhelpful or unconstructive cognitions. We shall call this a thought plan.

An example of an action plan for someone with a blood phobia rather like Clarissa's (see pp.67–8) could be:

1 To have my blood pressure taken.
2 To visit a hospital ward and remain there for several hours without fainting.
3 To have an injection.

4 To have a blood sample taken.
5 To give a pint of blood at the blood transfusion centre.

Each action plan will have to be tailor-made to the specific kind of phobia you have. Here is another example of an action plan. This time it is for dog phobia (see pp.53–4):

1 To be in a room with a dog and its owner with the dog on a leash.
2 To be in a room with the dog and its owner, with the dog off a leash.
3 To touch the dog in this situation.
4 To remain alone in the room with the dog when its owner leaves for a short while.
5 To visit public parks where dogs are.

At the same time as dealing with the behavioural problem using the action plan, the cognitive side has to be addressed using the thought plan. Once again, it has to be tailor-made to your own problem and should be worked out in detail. Using the example of the blood phobia, ask yourself what is the worst thing you think could happen to you if you had a blood sample taken. Then write down the answers on the right-hand side of a piece of paper, with headings at the top of the sheet: PHOBIA and ANSWERS. Some patients find it a difficult task to write down the answers but it is not impossible. The end result may be something like this:

1A If I have blood taken I will faint.
1B As I have never fainted when I had a blood test in the past, it is unlikely that I will now.
2A If I have a blood test I will make a fool of myself.
2B People who take blood from patients in hospital are used to people like me and will know how to treat me, so I really don't have to worry.
3A If I have a blood test I will die of fright.
3B It is the fear itself I am afraid of: no one dies of fear.

As well as this exercise in controlling your thoughts, it is helpful to devise ways of testing out long-held beliefs about your phobia. Getting as much information as possible is often useful: if you have a specific animal phobia I suggest you read about the animal species you are afraid of. One patient with a spider phobia learned in this way that there are no poisonous species of spider in the UK. Look at pictures of the animal or visit a natural history museum. This is easy for some patients but difficult for others. Become an expert on the animal you are afraid of. One patient learned the Latin names of all the species of spiders in the UK and this seemed to help her with the phobia.

What can you do if your phobia is something as intangible as a thunder or illness phobia? In these situations the thought plan may be the only possible approach. One such plan for illness phobia, which you can adopt as a starting-point for your own problem, might be:

1A This headache means I have a brain tumour.

1B As I have had the headache for twenty-five years on and off, I think if it were a tumour I would be dead by now.

2A I should go to my doctor for another check-up.

2B When I went last week the doctor gave me a thorough check-up and found nothing wrong then – or the time before that. Perhaps I am beginning to get into the habit of needing reassurance.

3A How can I be certain I have not got a physical disease?

3B You can never be *certain* of anything in life. You have to learn to live with some degree of risk. You even take a risk crossing the road to the doctor's surgery, but, after sensible precautions, you cross the road. If you have had a reasonable number of medical tests, just assume that you are most unlikely to have a brain tumour. You do not want to waste the rest of your life going to doctors and having tests.

Coping with setbacks

Self-help along these lines is often very effective for a variety of specific phobias. But some patients get upset when they find themselves slipping back and losing their original gains. If this happens, do not assume the worst and think you are back to square one. Human beings are not machines and to fail some-times is human. Most of us have off-days; do try to work out the reason for your off-day. Some women find it to be at the predictable time of their menstrual cycle. For both sexes, what psychiatrists call a life event could be happening. Remember that a life event can be a happy occasion, such as a birthday, or a clearly stressful event such as losing your job or a loved one. Whatever the life event you have isolated, remind yourself that it could be the cause of your relapse. You may need specific help such as counselling for the loss of a loved one. The important thing to remember is that you should expect the phobia to get worse at this time. Once you have come to terms with the event, then carry on with your action and thought plans as before.

The role of partner and family

As the partner of a phobic person is more likely to be a man, I shall continue to refer to *him*, but, as before, it could, of course, be a woman who is the partner of the sufferer. Giving the right kind of help is crucial as you saw with the husband of the snake phobic patient, Sally (see pp.49–52). He had to check all his wife's reading material to make certain that she did not come across a snake, and he swept the front path of the house after it rained in case there should be any worms on the path. He was being a kind and considerate husband. Or was he? The problem here is that his concern was tending to make his wife's phobia worse. Could you be acting in a similar way?

In general terms encouraging your partner to confront her phobia is a good idea. If she is trying hard but failing, think how you can help her face the situation. Criticism can provoke confrontation between you and working out a compromise is usually better than rigid rules. Take the example of a spider phobia where the husband has been given the job of removing spiders from the bath and has done so for many years. If he uses the modern approach to psychological treatment, he might sud-denly stop doing this, thereby causing his wife great distress. Instead, the couple could negotiate a compromise where he still removes the spiders but she tries to stay in the bathroom instead of running out in alarm. Later, he could put the spider in a jam jar with the lid firmly on and she could remove it herself.

I am often asked if getting a dog would help to cure a dog phobia. Once again, it is a question for individual discussion and negotiation. But do not simply buy a dog to see if it works out. Try gradual exposure to a neighbour's dog if it is of a gentle nature. In some cases patients then go on to own a dog although many never would.

The effect on children

I am also asked about the effect a wife's phobia might have on her children as, in some cases, this anxiety is the main reason for seeking therapy. Is it wise to seek help for this reason?

Studies have shown that children are less likely to develop fears if a trusted, reassuring adult is with them than if they meet the fearful stimulus alone. Support for the idea that fears are learned is given from studies of pre-school children in London air-raids: these showed that the children were more afraid of air-raids if their mothers showed fear than if they did not. If a small child regularly sees its mother jumping on a table when she catches sight of a small rodent, or running away when she sees a dog in the park, it could easily develop a similar problem. So, seeking help as an adult could be of benefit to your children. The important thing is how you *show* the fear and whether avoidance is seen to be accepted behaviour. Honesty is the best policy here and it is no use hiding the true facts. Explain that you do not like dogs but realize that this is silly and something you would like to change. Encourage your children to behave normally to dogs but do not allow them to bring their friends' dogs into your house without working out a plan of how to control them. In an ideal situation your children can help by encouraging the action plan of gradually facing up to dogs. These ideas can be applied to phobias of most domestic pets and of other animals.

In brief

- Use the action plan to devise a way of gradually facing up to what you are phobic about. It will take time to achieve progress but remember that practice makes perfect.

• Use the thought plan to teach you to say to yourself what helps you cope better. Remember that anxiety is unpleasant but does no harm.

• The role of your partner and family is important and often crucial. Remember that praise from a partner is better than criticism.

• Specific techniques such as relaxation and breathing help with panic attacks.

• The use of information through books about animals can be very helpful for animal phobias to test out whether your worst fears are founded on fact or whether you are misinformed.

• You are not alone with your phobia: join a self-help group.

Relaxation instructions

If you find that anxiety builds up just before you try to go out on a practice exercise, then work through these relaxation instructions beforehand. Some people even take a portable tape-recorder with them to play the instructions when they face the feared situation.

Settle back in your chair as comfortably as you can with your legs supported on a stool ... Start with the relaxation of your arms ... This begins with the contraction of the right biceps muscle ... Hold the contraction of the biceps for a few moments now (*about seven seconds*). Now relax your biceps by gradually straightening out your arm and resting it on the armrest of the chair ... Now focus on the feeling of relaxation in that muscle ... Try to think of your right biceps and nothing else for the moment (*about fifteen seconds*). Next contract your forearm muscles ... Do this by making a fist with your right hand and holding it (*about seven seconds*). Now let your fingers gradually straighten out and rest your hand over the armrest of the chair ... Focus now on the feeling of relaxation in your forearm and hand (*about fifteen seconds*). Now repeat these exercises for the other arm so that both arms become completely relaxed (*repeat as above for the left arm*).

Now carry on with the relaxation of your face and neck.
Begin with the scalp muscles at the top of your head ...
Contract these by raising your eyebrows towards the ceiling and
holding it for a short while. Now let your eyebrows go back to
the resting position and concentrate instead on the feeling of
relaxation in your scalp (*about fifteen seconds*). Now think of the
muscles to close your eyes and activate these by closing your
eyes (*about seven seconds*). Now let your eyelids relax so that
they are kept closed by their weight alone ... Concentrate on
this feeling of relaxation (*about fifteen seconds*). Next concentrate
on the muscles used to close your jaws and activate these by
closing your jaws tightly (*about seven seconds*). Now let your jaw
go completely slack and concentrate on that ... Check that you
are not contracting your jaw by exploring with your tongue that
your teeth are just a few millimetres apart (*wait about fifteen
seconds*). Now think of the large muscles at the back of your
neck ... Contract these by pushing your head into the backrest
of the chair (*about seven seconds*) ... Now let these muscles
relax by just letting your head remain there with the force of
gravity alone and concentrate on that (*about fifteen seconds*).

Now relax your chest and abdomen muscles. Begin by taking
in a deep breath and hold it (*about five seconds*) and then slowly
breathe out, relaxing as you do so. Now repeat this slow breathing a few times.

To contract your abdominal muscles imagine you are punch-
ing yourself in the tummy ... This makes you pull in these
muscles ... Hold that contraction (*about five seconds*). Now let
these muscles go slack and concentrate on that feeling for a few
moments (*about fifteen seconds*).

Next concentrate on your thighs and calves, followed by
complete body relaxation. Begin by raising your right leg off the
footstool with the knee straight ... keep it about three inches
above the stool (*about five seconds*) ... Now lower your leg
slowly and then concentrate on the feeling of relaxation at the
top of your thigh (*about fifteen seconds*). Next contract your calf
muscle on the right leg by pulling up your foot so that your toes
go up towards your head ... Hold that contraction for a few
moments (*about five seconds*). Now let your foot drop back to the

resting position and concentrate on the relaxation in that calf muscle (*about fifteen seconds*) (*repeat as above for the left leg*).

Keep relaxing your whole body now.

Next take slow, easy breaths . . . and check that your abdomen is completely relaxed. Now check the muscles at the top of your right leg . . . Now the calf on the right-hand side. Now do the same with the other leg starting with the thigh . . . And then the calf on the left-hand side. Your whole body should now be completely relaxed . . .

Reading List

For problems often related to phobias

Coping with Depression, Ivy Blackburn, Chambers, 1987.

Helplessness: On Depression, Development and Death, Martin Seligman, W. H. Freeman, 1992.

Feeling Good Handbook: Using the New Mood Therapy, David Burns, Plume, 1994.

Peace from Nervous Suffering, Claire Weekes, Angus & Robertson, 1990.

More Help for Your Nerves, Claire Weekes, Angus & Robertson, 1984.

Cognitive Therapy and the Emotional Disorders, Aaron Beck, Penguin Books, 1991.

The Boy Who Couldn't Stop Washing: The Experience and Treatment of Obsessive-compulsive Disorder, Judith Rapoport, Fontana, 1990.

Human Sexuality, Leonore Tiefer, Harper & Row, 1979.

The Joy of Sex, Alex Comfort, Quartet Books, 1976.

Families and How to Survive Them, Robin Skynner and John Cleese, Methuen, 1983.

Advice Sources

United Kingdom

1 Your general practitioner
2 Via your general practitioner you may be referred to local psychiatric or psychology services
3 The Phobic Society, 4 Cheltenham Road, Chorlton-cum-Hardy, Manchester M21 1QN Tel: 0161-881-1937
4 Phobic Action, Claybury Grounds, Manor Road, Woodford Green, Essex IG8 8PR Tel: 0181-559-2551 Helpline: 0181-559-2459
5 The Thanet Phobic Group, 47 Orchard Road, Westbrook, Margate, Kent CT9 5JS
6 Relaxation for Living, 168–170 Oatlands Drive, Weybridge, Surrey KT13 9ET Tel: 01932-831000
7 Triumph over Phobia (TOP UK), a self-help group run by phobic people to help each other: Celia Bonham Christie, 4 Marlborough Buildings, Bath BA1 2LX Tel: 01225 314129

United States

1 White Plains Hospital Phobia Clinic, 41 East Post Road, White Plains, New York, NY 10601
2 Institute for Behavior Therapy, 137 East 36th Street, New York, NY 10016
3 The Behavior Therapy Center of New York, 115 East 87th Street, New York, NY 10028
4 Payne Whitney Clinic Behavioral Services, New York Hospital, 525 East 68th Street, New York, NY 10021
5 Long Island Jewish Hospital at Hillside Phobia Clinic, New Hyde Park, New York, NY 11040
6 California Terrap, Arthur B Hardy MD, 1010 Doyle Street, Menlo Park, California 94025

Notes

There is an ever-increasing number of scientific journals and books on phobias and these notes are to guide readers who wish to pursue the literature. There are specialist journals notably in behaviour therapy: *Behaviour Research and Therapy* and *Behaviour Therapy*; and in psychiatry there are the *British Journal of Psychiatry* and *Archives of General Psychiatry*. In recent years the number of articles on phobias seems to have increased in an exponential way so that it is almost impossible to keep pace.

There are some outstanding books on phobias. One of these is *Fears, Phobias and Rituals* by Isaac Marks, Professor of Experimental Psychopathology at the Institute of Psychiatry, University of London (Oxford University Press, 1987). A scholarly book on agoraphobia is *Agoraphobia: Nature and Treatment* by Andrew Mathews, Michael Gelder and Derek Johnston (Tavistock Press, 1981). *The Practice of Behavioural and Cognitive Psychotherapy*, co-authored by me with L. D. Drummond (Cambridge University Press, 1991), is mainly for those who want to train in behavioural and cognitive methods as it describes the application of these methods to a variety of problems, including phobias.

The following references for points raised in individual chapters may help the academic reader.

1 Phobia: The Irrational Fear

1. Studies carried out on specific phobias:

Watson, J. P. and Marks, I. M. (1971). 'Relevant and irrelevant fear in flooding: A crossover study of phobic patients'. *Behaviour Therapy*, 2, pp.275–93.

Watson, J. P., Gaind, R. and Marks, I. M. (1972). 'Physiological habituation to continuous phobic stimulation'. *Behaviour Research and Therapy*, 10, pp.269–78.

2. References to systematic desensitization:

Wolpe, J. and Lazarus, A. A. (1966). *Behaviour Therapy Techniques: A Guide to the Treatment of Neurosis*. Pergamon Press.

Wolpe, J. (1958). *Psychotherapy by Reciprocal Inhibition*. Stanford University Press.

3. Study of agoraphobia where two hours' exposure was compared with thirty-minute sessions:

Stern, R. S. and Marks, I. M. (1973). 'Brief and prolonged flooding: a comparison in agoraphobic patients'. *Archives of General Psychiatry*, 28, pp.270–76.

4. Imipramine and behavioural treatment:

Marks, I. M., Gray, S., Cohen, D., Hill, R., Mawson, D., Ramm, E. and Stern, R. (1983). 'Imipramine and brief therapist-aided exposure in agoraphobics having self-exposure homework'. *Archives of General Psychiatry*, 40, pp.153–62.

5. Group therapy:

Hand, I., Lamontagne, Y. and Marks, I. M. (1974). 'Group exposure (flooding) *in vivo* for agoraphobia'. *British Journal of Psychiatry*, 124, pp.588–602.

6. Marital factors:

Hafner, R. J. (1977). 'The husbands of agoraphobic women and their influence on treatment and outcome'. *British Journal of Psychiatry*, 131, pp.289–94.

7. Philosophy of science:

Popper, Karl (1963). *Conjectures and Refutations*. Routledge & Kegan Paul.

Kuhn, T. H. (1970). *The Structure of Scientific Revolutions*. University of Chicago Press.

8. Rational emotive therapy:

Ellis, Albert (1962). *Reason and Emotion in Psychotherapy*. Citadel Press.

9. Cognitive therapy for anxiety:

Beck, A. T. and Emery G. (1985). *Anxiety Disorders and Phobias*. Basic Books.

10. Natural course of phobias:

Marks, I. and Herst, E. (1970). 'A survey of 1200 agoraphobics in Britain'. *Social Psychiatry*, 5, pp.16–24.

Buglass, D., Clarke, J., Henderson, A. S., Kreitman, N. and Presley, A. S. (1977). 'A study of agoraphobic housewives'. *Psychological Medicine*, 7, pp.73–86.

11. Articles on the prevalence of phobias:

Agras, S., Sylvester, D. and Oliveau, D. (1969). 'The epidemiology of common fears and phobias'. *Comprehensive Psychiatry*, 10, pp.151–6.

Weissman, M. M., Leaf, P. J., Holzer, C. E. and Merikangas, K. R. (1985). 'Epidemiology of anxiety disorders'. *Psychopharmaceutical Bulletin*, 26, pp.543–5.

Markowitz, J. S., Weissman, M. M., Ouellette, R., Lish, J. D. and Klerman, G. L. (1989). 'Quality of life in panic disorder'. *Archives of General Psychiatry*, 46, pp.984–92.

12. Genetic literature:

Carey, G. (1982). 'Genetic influences on anxiety neurosis and agoraphobia'. In Mathew R. J. (ed.), *The biology of anxiety*, pp.37–50. Brunner/Mazel.

Harris, E. L., Noyes, R., Crowe, R. R. and Chaudry, D. R. (1983). 'A family study of agoraphobia: a pilot study'. *Archives of General Psychiatry*, 40, pp.1061–4.

Moran, C. and Andrews, G. (1985). 'The familial occurrence of agoraphobia'. *British Journal of Psychiatry*, 146, pp.262–7

Solyom, L., Beck, P., Solyom, C. and Hugel, R. (1974). 'Some aetiological factors in phobic neurosis'. *Journal of the Canadian Psychiatric Association*, 19, pp.69–78.

Berg, I. (1976). 'School phobia in children of agoraphobic women'. *British Journal of Psychiatry*, 128, pp.86–9.

Torgersen, S. (1983). 'Genetics of neurosis: The effects of sampling variation upon the twin concordance ratio'. *British Journal of Psychiatry*, 142, pp.126–32.

Marks, I. M. (1969). *Fears and Phobias*. Academic Press.

13. Phobic anxiety depersonalization syndrome:

Roth, M. (1959). 'The phobic-anxiety-depersonalization syndrome'. *Proceedings of the Royal Society of Medicine*, 52, 8, p.587.

14. Generalized anxiety:

Weissman, M. M., Leaf, P. J., Holzer, C. E. and Merikangas, K. R. (1985). 'Epidemiology of anxiety disorders'. *Psychopharmaceutical Bulletin*, 26, pp.543–5.

15. Freud's description of Frau Emmy von N.:

Freud, Sigmund and Breuer, Joseph (1955, 1974). *Studies on Hysteria*. (Trans. James and Alix Strachey). Hogarth Press, Penguin Freud Library.

See also:

Wolpe, J. and Rachman, S. (1960). 'Psychoanalytic "evidence". A critique based on Freud's case of Little Hans'. *Journal of Nervous and Mental Disease*. 130, pp.135–8.

16. Fenichel on Freud:

Fenichel, O. (1944). 'Remarks on the common phobias'. *Psychoanalytical Quarterly*, 13, pp.313–26.

17. Baum box learning experiments on rats:

Baum, M. (1969). 'Extinction of an avoidance response following response prevention'. *Canadian Journal of Psychology*. 23, pp.1–10.

Lederhendler, I. and Baum, M. (1970). 'Mechanical facilitation of the action of response prevention (flooding) in rats'. *Behaviour Research and Therapy*, 8, pp.43–8.

2 Agoraphobia

1. Westphal, C. (1871). 'Die Agoraphobie: eine neuropathische erscheinung'. *Arch. fur Psychiatrie und Nervenkrankheiten*, 3, pp.138–71.

2. Some studies of imipramine in agoraphobia:

Marks, I. M. and O'Sullivan, G. (1988). 'Drugs and psychological treatments for agoraphobia/panic and obsessive-compulsive disorders: a review'. *British Journal of Psychiatry*, 153, pp.650–58.

Marks, I. M., Gray, S., Cohen, D., Hill, R., Mawson, D., Ramm, E. and Stern, R. (1983). 'Imipramine and brief therapist-aided exposure in agoraphobics having self-exposure homework'. *Archives of General Psychiatry*, 40, pp.153–62.

Zitrin, C. M., Klein, D. F. and Woerner, M. G. (1980). 'Treatment of agoraphobia with group exposure *in vivo* and imipramine'. *Archives of General Psychiatry*, 37, pp.63–72.

3. Failures of behavioural treatment:

Foa, Edna and Emmelkamp, Paul (1983). *The Failures of Behaviour Therapy*. John Wiley.

3 Social Phobias

1. Shepherd, G. (1983). Chapter 1 'Introduction'. In Spence, S. and Shepherd, G. (eds.) *Developments in Social Skills Training*. Academic Press.

   Solyom, L., Ledwidge, B. and Solyom, C. (1986). 'Delineating social phobia'. *British Journal of Psychiatry*, 149, pp.464–70.

   Stravynski, A., Marks, I. M. and Yule, W. (1982). 'Social skills problems in neurotic outpatients'. *Archives of General Psychiatry*, 39, pp.1378–85.

   Wlazlo, Z., Schroeder-Hartwig, Hand, I. *et al* (1990). 'Exposure *in vivo* vs social skills training for social phobia: long-term outcome and differential effects'. *Behaviour Research and Therapy*, 28, pp.181–93.

2. Frankl, Viktor E., 'Paradoxical Intention' and work originally published in Vienna 1946, available in translation:

   —*The Doctor and the Soul* (1973). Pelican Books.

   —*Psychotherapy and Existentialism* (1973). Pelican Books.

   Some books on social phobias and development of social skills mainly for sufferers:

   Garner, A. (1980). *Conversationally Speaking*. McGraw-Hill.

   Kleinke, C. L. (1986). *Meeting and Understanding People*. W. H. Freeman.

   General books on social phobias mainly of academic interest:

   Priestley, P., McGuire, J., Flegg, D., Hemsley, V. and Welham, D. (1978). *Social Skills and Personal Problem Solving*. Tavistock.

   Trower, P., Bryant, B. and Argyle, M. (1978). *Social Skills and Mental Health*. Methuen.

4 Animal Phobias

General references:

Marks, I. M. (1973). 'The reduction of fear: Towards a unifying theory'. *Journal of the Canadian Psychiatric Association*, 18, pp.9–12.

—(1981). *Cure and Care of Neurosis*. New York: Wiley.

—(1986). *Behavioural Psychotherapy*. Bristol: Wright.

Stern, R. S. (1978). *Behavioural Techniques*. Academic Press.

Watson, J. P. and Marks, I. M. (1971). 'Relevant and irrelevant fear in flooding: A crossover study of phobic patients'. *Behaviour Therapy*, 2, pp.275–93.

5 Various Phobias

1. Classification of phobias:

Hunter, Richard and Macalpine, Ida (1963). *Three Hundred Years of Psychiatry*. Oxford University Press.

For modern ideas on classification see *The ICD–10 Classification of Mental and Behavioural Disorders* (1992), published by the World Health Organization. This volume states aptly that 'a classification is a way of seeing the world at a point in time'. Phobic anxiety disorders are divided into agoraphobia (with or without panic disorder), social phobias and specific isolated phobias.

2. Space phobia:

Marks, I. M. and Bebbington, P. (1976). 'Space phobia: syndrome or agoraphobic variant?'. *British Medical Journal*, 2, pp.345–7.

3. Benedikt, M. (1870). *Allgemeine Wiener Medizinische Zeitung*, 15, pp.488.

4. Janet, P. (1903). *Les Obsessions et la Psychasthenie*. Paris: Baillière.

Translations are available for most of his work, for example:

—(1925). *Psychological Healing*. (trans. Eden and Cedar Paul). George Allen & Unwin.

5. Marks, I. M. (1987). *Fears, Phobias and Rituals*. Oxford University Press.

6 Sexual Phobias

1. Comfort, Alex (1976). *The Joy of Sex*. Quartet Books.

2. Masters, W. H. and Johnson, V. E. (1966). *Human Sexual Response*. Churchill.

—(1970). *Human Sexual Inadequacy*. Churchill.

General references for sexual and marital problems:

Bancroft, J. (1983). *Human Sexuality and Its Problems*. Churchill Livingstone.

Crowe, M. J. (1978). 'Conjoint marital therapy: a controlled outcome study'. *Psychological Medicine*, 8, pp.623–36.

Crowe, M. J., Gillan, P., and Golombok, S. (1981). 'Form and content in the conjoint treatment of sexual dysfunction: a controlled study'. *Behaviour Research and Therapy*, 19, pp.47–54.

Delvin, D. (1974). *The Book of Love*. New English Library.

Friedman, D. (1968). 'The treatment of impotence by brietal relaxation therapy'. *Behaviour Research and Therapy*, 6, pp.257–61.

Haslam, M. T. (1965). 'The treatment of psychogenic dyspareunia by reciprocal inhibition'. *British Journal of Psychiatry*, 111, pp.280–82.

Hawton, K. (1985). *Sex Therapy: A Practical Guide*. Oxford University Press.

Jacobson, N. (1981). 'Behavioural marital therapy'. In *Handbook of Family Therapy*. A. S. Gurman and D. P. Kniskern (eds.). Brunner/Mazel Inc., New York.

Jacobson, N. S. and Gurman, A. S. (1986). *Clinical Handbook of Marital Therapy*. New York: Guilford Press.

Kaplan, H. S. (1976). *The Illustrated Manual of Sex Therapy*. Souvenir Press.

Lazarus, A. A. (1963). 'The treatment of chronic frigidity by systematic desensitization'. *Journal of Nervous and Mental Disorders*, 136, pp.272–8.

Marquis, J. N. (1970). 'Orgasmic reconditioning: Changing sexual object choice through controlling masturbation fantasies'. *Journal of Behaviour Therapy and Experimental Psychiatry*, 1, pp.263–70.

Semans, J. M. (1956). 'Premature Ejaculation: a new approach'. *Southern Medical Journal*, 49, pp.353–7.

Stuart, R. B. (1969). 'Operant-interpersonal treatment for marital discord'. *Journal of Consulting and Clinical Psychology*. 33, pp.675–82.

Stuart, R. B. (1973). *Premarital Counselling Inventory*. Champaign, Ill.: Research Press.

Stuart, R. B. (1980). *Helping Couples Change*. New York: Guilford Press.

Zilbergeld, B. (1980) *Men and Sex*, Fontana.

7 Misconceptions

1. For depressive illness see:

Beck, A. T., Rush, J. A., Shaw, B. F. and Emery, G. (1979). *Cognitive Therapy of Depression*. New York: Guilford Press.

Blackburn, I. M. (1987). *Coping with Depression*. Chambers.

Blackburn, I. M., Funson, K. M. and Bishop, S. (1986). 'A two-year naturalistic follow-up of depressed patients treated with cognitive therapy, pharmacotherapy and a combination of both'. *Journal of Affective Disorders*, 10, pp.67–75.

Elkin, I., Shea, T., Watkins, J. T., Imber, S. D., *et al.* (1989). 'National Institute of Mental Health treatment of depression collaborative research program'. *Archives of General Psychiatry*, 46, pp.971–82.

Lewinsohn, P. M. (1975). 'Behavioral Study and Treatment of Depression'. In *Progress in Behavior Modification*, vol.1, R. M. Eisler and P. M. Miller (eds.). New York: Academic Press.

Lewinsohn, P. M. and Graf, M. (1973). 'Pleasant activities and depression'. *Journal of Consulting and Clinical Psychology*, 41, pp.261–8.

Seligman, M. E. P. (1975). *On Depression, Development and Death*. San Francisco: W. H. Freeman.

Simons, A. D., Murphy, G. E., Levine, J. L., *et al.* (1986). 'Cognitive therapy and pharmacotherapy for Depression'. *Archives of General Psychiatry*, 43, pp.43–50.

Sireling, L., Cohen, D. and Marks, I. (1988). 'Guided mourning for morbid grief: A controlled replication'. *Behaviour Therapy*, 19, pp.121–32.

Weissman, M. M. and Paykel, E. S. (1974). *The Depressed Woman*. University of Chicago Press.

2. For obsessive-compulsive disorder see:

Marks, I. M. (1987). *Fears, Phobias and Rituals*. Oxford University Press.

Marks, I. M., Hodgson, R. and Rachman, S. (1975). 'Treatment of chronic OCD two years after *in vivo* exposure'. *British Journal of Psychiatry*, 127, pp.349–64.

Marks, I. M., Lelliot, P., Basoglu, M., Noshirvani, H., Monteiro, W., Cohen, D. and Kasvikis, Y. (1988). 'Clomipramine, self-exposure and therapist-aided exposure for obsessive-compulsive rituals'. *British Journal of Psychiatry*, 152, pp.522–34.

Rachman, S., Hodgson, R. and Marks, I. M. (1971). 'Treatment of chronic obsessive-compulsive neurosis'. *Behaviour Research and Therapy*, 9, pp.237–47.

Stern, R. S. (1978). 'Obsessive thoughts: The problem of therapy'. *British Journal of Psychiatry*, 132, pp.200–205.

Stern, R. S. and Cobb, J. P. (1978). 'Phenomenology of obsessive-compulsive neurosis'. *British Journal of Psychiatry*, 132, pp.233–9.

8 The Role of Medication

1. Most patients are very worried about medication and reading about it seems to make the anxiety worse. Information in such works as the *British National Formulary* (published annually in London by the British Medical Association) has to include every possible side-effect of a drug. Reading this list can be very disturbing although many of the drugs are relatively safe. I have tried to address this problem in chapter 8, but the reader may like to explore this literature further.

Gray, J. A. (1987). 'Interaction between drugs and behaviour therapy'. In *Theoretical Foundations of Behaviour Therapy*. Eysenck, H. J. and Martin, I. (eds.). New York: Plenum.

Hafner, R. J. and Marks, I. M. (1976). 'Exposure *in vivo* of agoraphobics: Contribution of diazepam, group exposure, and anxiety evocation'. *Psychological Medicine*, 6, pp.71–88.

Klein, D. F. (1964). 'Delineation of two drug responsive anxiety syndromes'. *Psychopharmacologia*, 5, pp.397–408.

Marks, I. M., Gray, S., Cohen, D., Hill, R., Mawson, D., Ramm, E. and Stern, R. (1983). 'Imipramine and brief therapist-aided exposure in agoraphobics having self-exposure homework'. *Archives of General Psychiatry*, 40, pp.153–62.

Marks, I. M. and O'Sullivan, G. (1988). 'Drugs and psychological treatments for agoraphobia/panic and obsessive-compulsive disorders: a review'. *British Journal of Psychiatry*, 153, pp.650–58.

Nagy, L. M., Krystal, J. H., Woods, S. W. and Charney, D. S. (1989). 'Clinical and medication outcome after short-term Alprazolam and behavioural group treatment in panic disorder'. *Archives of General Psychiatry*, 46, pp.993–9.

Noyes, R., Anderson, D. J., Clancy, J. *et al.* (1984). 'Diazepam and propranolol in panic disorder and agoraphobia'. *Archives of General Psychiatry*, 41, pp.287–92.

Telch, M. J., Agras, W. S., Taylor, C. B., Roth, W. T. and Gallen, C. G. (1985). 'Combined pharmacological and behavioural treatment for agoraphobia'. *Behaviour Research and Therapy*, 23, pp.325–34.

Tyrer, P., Candy, J. and Kelly, D. (1973). 'Phenelzine in phobic anxiety: a controlled trial'. *Psychological Medicine*, 3, pp.120–24.

Wardle, J. (1990). 'Behaviour therapy and benzodiazepines: allies or antagonists?' *British Journal of Psychiatry*, 156, pp.163–8.

Zitrin, C. M., Klein, D. F. and Woerner, M. G. (1980). 'Treatment of agoraphobia with Group Exposure *in vivo* and imipramine'. *Archives of General Psychiatry*, 37, pp.63–72.

Index

READ MORE IN PENGUIN

In every corner of the world, on every subject under the sun, Penguin represents quality and variety – the very best in publishing today.

For complete information about books available from Penguin – including Puffins, Penguin Classics and Arkana – and how to order them, write to us at the appropriate address below. Please note that for copyright reasons the selection of books varies from country to country.

In the United Kingdom: Please write to *Dept. JC, Penguin Books Ltd, FREEPOST, West Drayton, Middlesex UB7 0BR.*

If you have any difficulty in obtaining a title, please send your order with the correct money, plus ten per cent for postage and packaging, to *PO Box No. 11, West Drayton, Middlesex UB7 0BR*

In the United States: Please write to *Consumer Sales, Penguin USA, P.O. Box 999, Dept. 17109, Bergenfield, New Jersey 07621-0120.* VISA and MasterCard holders call 1-800-253-6476 to order all Penguin titles

In Canada: Please write to *Penguin Books Canada Ltd, 10 Alcorn Avenue, Suite 300, Toronto, Ontario M4V 3B2*

In Australia: Please write to *Penguin Books Australia Ltd, P.O. Box 257, Ringwood, Victoria 3134*

In New Zealand: Please write to *Penguin Books (NZ) Ltd, Private Bag 102902, North Shore Mail Centre, Auckland 10*

In India: Please write to *Penguin Books India Pvt Ltd, 706 Eros Apartments, 56 Nehru Place, New Delhi 110 019*

In the Netherlands: Please write to *Penguin Books Netherlands bv, Postbus 3507, NL-1001 AH Amsterdam*

In Germany: Please write to *Penguin Books Deutschland GmbH, Metzlerstrasse 26, 60594 Frankfurt am Main*

In Spain: Please write to *Penguin Books S. A., Bravo Murillo 19, 1° B, 28015 Madrid*

In Italy: Please write to *Penguin Italia s.r.l., Via Felice Casati 20, I–20124 Milano*

In France: Please write to *Penguin France S. A., 17 rue Lejeune, F–31000 Toulouse*

In Japan: Please write to *Penguin Books Japan, Ishikiribashi Building, 2–5–4, Suido, Bunkyo-ku, Tokyo 112*

In Greece: Please write to *Penguin Hellas Ltd, Dimocritou 3, GR–106 71 Athens*

In South Africa: Please write to *Longman Penguin Southern Africa (Pty) Ltd, Private Bag X08, Bertsham 2013*

READ MORE IN PENGUIN

PSYCHOLOGY

Introduction to Jung's Psychology   Frieda Fordham

'She has delivered a fair and simple account of the main aspects of my psychological work. I am indebted to her for this admirable piece of work' – C. G. Jung in the Foreword

Child Care and the Growth of Love   John Bowlby

His classic 'summary of evidence of the effects upon children of lack of personal attention . . . presents to administrators, social workers, teachers and doctors a reminder of the significance of the family' – *The Times*

Recollections and Reflections   Bruno Bettelheim

'A powerful thread runs through Bettelheim's message: his profound belief in the dignity of man, and the importance of seeing and judging other people from their own point of view' – *Independent*. 'These memoirs of a wise old child, candid, evocative, heart-warming, suggest there is hope yet for humanity' – *Evening Standard*

Female Perversions   Louise J. Kaplan

'If you can't have love, what do you get? Perversion, be it mild or severe: shopping, seduction, anorexia or self-mutilation. Kaplan charts both Madame Bovary's "perverse performance" and the more general paths to female self-destruction with a grace, determination and intellectual firmness rare in the self-discovery trade. A most remarkable book' – Fay Weldon

The Psychology of Interpersonal Behaviour   Michael Argyle

Social behaviour and relationships with others are one of the main sources of happiness, but their failure may result in great distress and can be a root cause of mental illness. In the latest edition of this classic text, Michael Argyle has included the latest research on non-verbal communication, social skills and happiness, and has extensively revised and updated the text throughout.

READ MORE IN PENGUIN

PSYCHOLOGY

Psychoanalysis and Feminism Juliet Mitchell

'Juliet Mitchell has risked accusations of apostasy from her fellow feminists. Her book not only challenges orthodox feminism, however; it defies the conventions of social thought in the English-speaking countries . . . a brave and important book' – *New York Review of Books*

The Divided Self R. D. Laing

'A study that makes all other works I have read on schizophrenia seem fragmentary . . . The author brings, through his vision and perception, that particular touch of genius which causes one to say, "Yes, I have always known that, why have I never thought of it before?"' – *Journal of Analytical Psychology*

Water Logic Edward de Bono

Edward de Bono has always sought to provide practical thinking tools that are simple to use but powerful in action. Here he turns his attention to simplifying the thought processes when dealing with practical problems.

Cultivating Intuition Peter Lomas

Psychoanalytic psychotherapy is a particular kind of conversation, a shared project and process in which both participants can express their individuality and negotiate their rights. Here Peter Lomas explores the aims and qualities of that conversation between therapist and patient.

The Care of the Self Michel Foucault
The History of Sexuality Volume 3

Foucault examines the transformation of sexual discourse from the Hellenistic to the Roman world in an inquiry which 'bristles with provocative insights into the tangled liaison of sex and self' – *The Times Higher Education Supplement*

Mothering Psychoanalysis Janet Sayers

'An important book . . . records the immense contribution to psycho-analysis made by its founding mothers' – *Sunday Times*

READ MORE IN PENGUIN

A SELECTION OF HEALTH BOOKS

The Kind Food Guide   Audrey Eyton

Audrey Eyton's all-time bestselling *The F-Plan Diet* turned the nation on to fibre-rich food. Now, as the tide turns against factory farming, she provides the guide destined to bring in a new era of eating.

Baby and Child   Penelope Leach

This comprehensive, authoritative and practical handbook is an essential guide, with sections on every stage of the first five years of life.

Woman's Experience of Sex   Sheila Kitzinger

Fully illustrated with photographs and line drawings, this book explores the riches of women's sexuality at every stage of life. 'A book which any mother could confidently pass on to her daughter – and her partner too' – *Sunday Times*

The Effective Way to Stop Drinking   Beauchamp Colclough

Beauchamp Colclough is an international authority on drink dependency, a reformed alcoholic, and living proof that today's decision is tomorrow's freedom. Follow the expert advice contained here, and it will help you give up drinking – for good.

Living with Alzheimer's Disease and Similar Conditions
Dr Gordon Wilcock

This complete and compassionate self-help guide is designed for families and carers (professional or otherwise) faced with the 'living bereavement' of dementia.

Living with Stress
Cary L. Cooper, Rachel D. Cooper and Lynn H. Eaker

Stress leads to more stress, and the authors of this helpful book show why low levels of stress are desirable and how best we can achieve them in today's world. Looking at those most vulnerable, they demonstrate ways of breaking the vicious circle that can ruin lives.

READ MORE IN PENGUIN

A SELECTION OF HEALTH BOOKS

Living with Asthma and Hay Fever John Donaldson

For the first time, there are now medicines that can prevent asthma attacks from taking place. Based on up-to-date research, this book shows how the majority of sufferers can beat asthma and hay fever to lead full and active lives.

Anorexia Nervosa R. L. Palmer

Lucid and sympathetic guidance for those who suffer from this disturbing illness and their families and professional helpers, given with a clarity and compassion that will make anorexia more understandable and consequently less frightening for everyone involved.

Medicines: A Guide for Everybody Peter Parish

The use of any medicine is always a balance of benefits and risks – this book will help the reader understand how to extend the benefits and reduce the risks. Completely revised, it is written in ordinary, accessible language for the layperson, and is also indispensable to anyone involved in health care.

Other People's Children Sheila Kitzinger

Though step-families are common, adults and children in this situation often feel isolated because they fail to conform to society's idealized picture of a normal family. This sensitive, incisive book is essential reading for anyone involved with or in a step-family.

Miscarriage Ann Oakley, Ann McPherson and Helen Roberts

One million women worldwide become pregnant every day. At least half of these pregnancies end in miscarriage or stillbirth. But each miscarriage is the loss of a potential baby, and that loss can be painful to adjust to. Here is sympathetic support and up-to-date information on one of the commonest areas of women's reproductive experience.

READ MORE IN PENGUIN

A SELECTION OF HEALTH BOOKS

When a Woman's Body Says No to Sex   Linda Valins

Vaginismus – an involuntary spasm of the vaginal muscles that prevents penetration – has been discussed so little that many women who suffer from it don't recognize their condition by its name. Linda Valins's practical and compassionate guide will liberate these women from their fears and sense of isolation and help them find the right form of therapy.

Mixed Messages   Brigid McConville

Images of breasts – young and naked, sexual and chic – are everywhere. Yet for many women, the form, functions and health of our own breasts remain shrouded in mystery, ignorance – even fear. The consequences of our culture's breast taboos are tragic: Britain's breast-cancer death rate is the highest in the world. Every woman should read *Mixed Messages* – the first book to consider the well-being of our breasts in the wider contexts of our lives.

Defeating Depression   Tony Lake

Counselling, medication, and the support of friends can all provide invaluable help in relieving depression. But if we are to combat it once and for all, we must face up to perhaps painful truths about our past and take the first steps forward that can eventually transform our lives. This lucid and sensitive book shows us how.

Freedom and Choice in Childbirth   Sheila Kitzinger

Undogmatic, honest and compassionate, Sheila Kitzinger's book raises searching questions about the kind of care offered to the pregnant woman – and will help her make decisions and communicate effectively about the kind of birth experience she desires.

The Complete New Herbal   Richard Mabey

The new bible for herb users – authoritative, up-to-date, absorbing to read and hugely informative, with practical, clear sections on cultivation and the uses of herbs in daily life, nutrition and healing.